D1125012

CHURCH PLANTING
LANDMINES

MISTAKES to AVOID
in Years 2 through 10

TOM NEBEL AND GARY ROHRMAYER

Published by ChurchSmart Resources

We are an evangelical Christian publisher committed to producing excellent products at affordable prices to help church leaders accomplish effective ministry in the areas of Church planting, Church growth, Church renewal and Leadership Development.

For a free catalog of our resources call 1-800-253-4276.

Visit us at: www.churchsmart.com

Cover design by: Julie Becker

Manuscript edited by: Stuart Hoffman

© copyright 2005
   by Tom Nebel and Gary Rohrmayer

ISBN#: 1-889638-50-1

CHURCH PLANTING
LANDMINES

MISTAKES to AVOID
in Years 2 through 10

DEDICATION

This book is dedicated to Paul and Steve Johnson,
"The Sons of Thunder"

Remember your leaders, who spoke the Word of God to you.
Consider the outcome of their way of life and imitate their faith.
Hebrews 13:7

TABLE OF CONTENTS

INTRODUCTION

"Call us Stumpy!" Like Melville's mythical character Captain Ahab, floating on the high seas of church planting, we've experienced enough disasters (in pursuit of the great white whale of expanding God's Kingdom) that we walk with a limp. Some of our friends, when told of the title of this book, have said, "Oh, an autobiography!" They're right.

Tom Nebel and Gary Rohrmayer have known each other for nearly twenty years. When Tom and Lori Nebel planted Community Church in Whitewater, Wisconsin, in 1986 they had a dream of seeing daughter churches spring from that church. Along came Gary and Mary Rohrmayer, fresh out of Bible school, with the vision to plant that first daughter church. But even that's a bit of an exaggeration. Community Church in Whitewater gave the Rohrmayers $50 per month and one of our church families that was moving to the target community of Oconomowoc anyway. So with a pat on the back, the Rohrmayers pioneered this new church.

Tom and Gary are best of friends, but it wasn't always that way. When Tom served as Gary's church planting coach, they came to blows enough times that they, as they like to say, "hated each other in a loving, Christian-sort-of-way." Some of it was personality and immaturity, but some of it was landmines! In church planting, it seems that the battle doesn't really begin until the church gets started. Up until then it's mostly vision, dreams, and energy. War documentaries often tell of the soldiers, on the way to battle, laughing and taking it easy. They sing songs and write letters and expect to make it home alive. But then the real bullets start to fly, and the situation quickly changes. They see buddies fall. And they become wounded or even lost themselves. It's usually more invigorating to anticipate the battle than to participate in it.

The landmines we have encountered have left us with limps. But personal injuries aside, the genesis of this book lies in what they've seen during their years of leading church planting movements. There will always be casualties in the battles for the Kingdom, but so many mistakes can be avoided by thinking ahead and implementing strategies that really work. Thankfully, over the past couple of decades, gifted authors have given us wonderful materials on how to get a new church started. Our ministries are richer, broader, and deeper because of them. This book is offered to help the leaders of the now-planted church sail as smoothly as possible into years two through ten.

God bless you in your journey! And be careful where you step!

Dr. Tom Nebel
Great Lakes Church Planting
Madison, WI
tomnebel@aol.com
www.weplantchurches.com

Rev. Gary Rohrmayer
Midwest Church Planting
Chicago, IL
gary@midwestchurchplanting.net
www.midwestchurchplanting.net
www.yourjourney.org

FOREWORD

Bob (not his real name) was one of the top planters I had ever assessed. He was the "whole package." I was certain that he would do well. We approved him, encouraged him, funded him, and sent him out. He started with a flash but soon burned out. His family suffered; his personal life suffered; the church did not grow. I remember when he related to me what his wife had told him: "I am going home to South Carolina; I hope you are coming with me."

Bob's story illustrates the unpredictable and sometimes painful nature of starting a church. Church planting can be both the most exhilarating and exhausting task one can undertake. Highs and lows are common. The tendency is to focus on the highs and successes. But what about the pitfalls and land-mines of church planting? Successful planters and teams admit that success is often the result of experiencing numerous failures and learning from those failures. Therefore, it is crucial that current church planters learn from the failures of others so that they can avoid some of the church planting landmines.

Church planting is a highly demanding endeavor because it requires great faith and hard work. A church planter and the planting team are stretched and strained. The process of planting a church can squeeze every bit of time, energy, resources, and self-sufficiency out of the church planter and his or her family, with no guarantees of success. This strenuous endeavor can leave the church plant and the church planter vulnerable to church planting landmines.

The Pain of Church Planting Failure

I have been planting churches and working with church planters since 1988. During that time, I have contemplated the causes and nature of church-starting failures. In my mind, I can picture face after face of intelligent planters who I definitely thought would succeed. They were impressive, gifted, articulate, and passionate, but eventually they shipwrecked in ministry.

We don't like to talk about failures and the reasons for them. Maybe we are too proud to admit that we fall short of the task sometimes. Maybe we don't want to consider the harsh realities of ministry landmines. Looking the other way is easier. Planters and pastors who fail don't speak at our conferences or write books. We hold up the successes, and then wonder why our planters are surprised by hardships and overwhelmed by failure.

I have always been struck by the first few minutes of the movie *Saving Private Ryan*. The Americans have landed on the beach. Captain Miller (Tom Hanks) sees an opening for the men with protection on the other side. He says, "That's the route." Immediately, he sends six men through the gap who are brutally killed. The sergeant, who is more experienced, warns Miller with a stern look, "That's a #@! shooting gallery, Captain." Miller responds, "That's the route." Miller commands another group of six: "Go." They obey and are brutally cut down. Miller turns to the next six and says, "It's the only way. You're next." The third group of six loses several but finally breaks through the German lines. It is hard to watch; many people close their eyes, unable to stomach the harsh realities of combat.

That's what church planting looked like when I started back in the late 80s. Planters and their teams, unprepared for the challenges ahead, quickly ran into "harvest fields" that became "killing fields." They were enthusiastic but unprepared. They were excited for the task, but they were not ready to face the realities of church planting. Things have improved since then, but too many planters are still unprepared and ill-equipped for the task. Too many are still walking right into the landmines of church planting; they are often left broken and disillusioned—unable to comprehend and accept the harsh reality of failure and how to learn from its pain.

Tom Nebel and Gary Rohrmayer have provided a service to the church and her planters. As I read the book, I repeatedly thought, "They are right about that one." In almost every one of the cases, a former planter came to mind that fit the description, and I was grieved as I thought about each loss. But these losses can serve as the foundation for future church planting success if the courage exists to examine those failures. This book can spare many church planters and teams from stepping on the landmines of ministry—or at least prepare them to respond well when they hit one.

Learning from Failure

When we study international missions, we frequently consider failure—it helps avoid repeating past errors. Sometimes people fail at cross-cultural communication. Others fail because they syncretize the gospel. Sometimes missionaries fail to guard their hearts. Each failure should be a lesson for future leaders. This book is a guide for North American missions. By observing what went wrong with others, we will not be surprised and disheartened when those same landmines explode in our midst. Instead, we learn to expect the problem, and we gain insight into addressing it when it occurs.

Learning from failure is a key concept in life and successful church planting. When considering failure, we might think of Thomas Edison who failed hundreds of times before finally discovering the light bulb. However, his perspective was not clouded by failure. Edison considered each failure a learning process—he was just discovering all the ways not to produce the light bulb.

Over the centuries the church has experienced times of great success and times of great failure. Sometimes there was great momentum and forward movement, yet at other times the church lost ground or could not find a way to expand the kingdom among certain people groups. Missionaries did not always succeed in their task or find success quickly and easily. Success often came as the result of a process of experiencing failures and then learning from those failures. Church planting is no different today. It also needs to be seen as a process of "failing forward."

Thinking Ahead When You Are a Visionary Doer

By definition, church planters and teams are not particularly reflective; they are people of action who focus on the work of changing the world. Church planters don't like to think about the things that will stop them, just the things that will keep them going. I know this from personal experience; I have stepped on many of the landmines discussed in this book, including disregarding personal health, lack of leadership development, evangelism entropy in the church, underestimating spiritual warfare, and poor hiring decisions.

I wish that, as a first-time church planter, I could have read this book with my core team. However, I believe that reading it once would not be enough. This is the kind of book that needs to be read at least every few months, because problems can arise suddenly.

In addition, church planters are visionary. Not only do they want to avoid considering obstacles, but they also do not want to contemplate any negative possibilities. As visionaries, church planters often believe that things have become reality before they actually happen. Church planters need to engage in the church planting process with their eyes wide open to both the possibilities and the potential pitfalls. This book will help the visionary planter maintain a balanced, healthy perspective in the midst of the battle.

Doing It Better by Learning from Others

Church planting is more art than science. As with any missional endeavor, the church planter needs to stand on the edge of lostness. When you are there, the chance of failure is great, but so is the chance for great results. *Church Planting Landmines* is a vital resource that can increase the opportunity for achieving great results in church planting.

There is a climactic scene in the movie *Remember the Titans*. Coach Boone (Denzel Washington) leads his football team on a long, early-morning run to the battlefield of Gettysburg. In the early morning fog and mist, he challenges the team to set aside the landmine of racism and come together as a football team. He states, "Fifty thousand men died right here on this field. Fightin' the same fight that we're still fightin' amongst ourselves today. This green field right here—painted red, bubbling with the blood of young boys, smoke and hot lead going right through their bodies. Listen to their souls, men... . You listen and take a lesson from the dead. If we don't come together right now on this hallowed ground, we too will be destroyed just like they were."

Conclusion

Most of us don't listen well. I usually don't. Most of us have to learn by painful mistakes. Yet, those who God blesses most are those who listen best. This book could save your church plant. More importantly, it could save your marriage, your health, your ministry, and so on ... if you listen. Listen to the souls of those who have stepped on church planting landmines in the past. Listen and learn from their mistakes. God will use that wisdom to help you avoid the landmines of church planting. Keep failing forward!

— Ed Stetzer

Ed Stetzer is the author of many articles and books, including *Planting New Churches in a Postmodern Age*, Nashville: Broadman and Holman, 2003.

LANDMINE 1:

IGNORING PERSONAL HEALTH AND GROWTH

*As I see it, every day you do one of two things:
build health or produce disease in yourself.*
Adelle Davis

Quit worrying about your health. It'll go away.
Robert Orben

"**M**any start well, but few finish well." That's what Dr. Bobby Clinton, professor of leadership at Fuller Theological Seminary says. He bases his belief on research of thousands of Christian leaders, but you don't need to be an engineer and statistician to know that Clinton has his hands around something that's true. We've all seen leaders who have started the ministry race well—appearing to be on a life trajectory that would land them among the ministry elite. They would be the true difference-makers of their generation. But something happened. They burned out, they gave up, or they were disqualified.

At one time I didn't think that could happen to church planters. It seemed to me that church planters were not among those who were leaving ministry through things like moral failure. I made that observation to a friend of mine once, a fellow church planter. We both wondered what it was about church planters that made them so special that they didn't fall. Greater holiness? Greater commitment to the Lord and to the Cause? About a month later I saw my friend again, and each of us had stories to tell about church planters who had fallen. That shattered my theory.

Dr. Clinton has researched thousands of leaders, looking for the common denominators of those who "finish well." Clinton's Leadership Emergence Theory (*The Making of a Leader*, IVP, 1988) has been helpful to many growing leaders as they have sought perspective and guidance on their journey.

Because many start well but few finish well, leaders fall into one of three categories: (1) those who finish well, (2) those who finish "so-so," and (3) those who finish poorly. Clinton says that only about one third of Christian leaders finish well. And it would seem that the third category, those who finish poorly, would best describe derailment in the life of a leader. I've found Dr. Clinton's analogy of life being like a chess game to be helpful.

The Chess Game Analogy

Those who know something about chess refer to the opening game, the middle game, and the end game. In the opening game, moves are very standard. Pawn to Queen 4. Or Pawn to King's Bishop 4. They are standard opening moves. Even those who've just started playing chess know the standard opening moves. When my son Matthew was five years old, he knew how to start a game of chess well.

Before I go to the middle game, let me jump to the end game. The objective in chess is to defeat the opponent by capturing his or her king. When the king is unavoidably captured, it's called checkmate. You probably know that. But here's what's interesting. When young players play a game of chess they fight to the finish, systematically capturing more and more pieces until there are very few pieces left on the board. It's not unusual to see youngsters chasing each other around a board while one player has nothing other than a king, and the other player has only two or three combatants. That's how it works with rookie chess players; they go through the motions until someone wins.

But that's not the case with experienced players. Those who have been around the game long enough know that most of the pieces can still be on the board when the inevitable occurs and someone resigns. Notice that I said, "Someone resigns." Checkmating hardly ever occurs in competitive or tournament chess. When certain conditions exist, it's obvious to both players that it's simply a matter of time before the victim is checkmated. So rather than go through the motions, the loser tips over the king and resigns.

The point is this: in "real" chess, the end game hardly even exists. It's the middle game that counts the most. What happens in the middle game foretells what happens in the end game. And as in chess, finishing well as a leader is determined in the middle game.

If life is won or lost in the middle game, how is the middle game defined? According to Clinton's research, the middle game is the years between 35 and 55. Statistically speaking, people in ministry burn out, give up, or are disqualified most often between the ages of 35 and 55. In other words, if you are younger than 35 and haven't lost the game yet, don't be deceived into thinking that you're bullet-proof. The fact is that that train just hasn't come down your tracks yet—at least the way it will. But the good news is that if you're older than 55 and are on a course to finish well, you probably will. A few years back I was teaching on this subject at a conference, and my roommate was Dick Young, a church planter from Cheyenne, Wyoming. Dick was 57 at the time. One day, when he had finished showering, he laughed and said, "You know, Tom, I've never stolen a hotel towel, and I probably never will!" That's right.

I want to explain how finishing well plays out in new church situations. Let me begin with a hypothesis: church planters are vulnerable in a unique way because they have more freedom than established church pastors do when it comes to the creation of policy and protocol. Why? Because church planters "get there first." They are the lone and most qualified expert, so their influence is superior to all others.

This was made real to me many years ago when I was visiting a friend who was pastoring in a church that was over 115 years old. It was one of those churches with the "wall of fame"—the wall with the sequential display of all of the church's pastors down through the years. My friend, Scott, had his picture at the end of the line. He showed me the picture, but then he took me to the hall storage closet, where there was a stack of perhaps a dozen picture frames! Someone along the line had figured out that pastors are employees. They come and go, so we might as well get symmetrical picture frames! In churches like that, the pastor can expect to have a limited amount of influence in establishing policy and protocol.

The situation is very different in most church plants, where the church planters have broad freedoms. If the church is going well, the members can't imagine a future without the church planter; there will be no early rush to buy symmetrical picture frames. However, with freedom comes the responsibility to guard against common race-enders.

Common Race-Enders

1. The Abuse of Finances

Ministry and money are mysteriously wed together, and it's hard to imagine ministry occurring without money playing a prominent role. When the proper set of circumstances occurs, even the most unlikely ministers can be tempted in this arena. Strange things happen to church planters, too, when it comes to money. I know of one church planter who had full control over the finances of his young church. He deposited the offerings and paid the bills. And after about six months of ministry, he decided to give himself a raise, because "if I had a church board, they would have given me a raise by now." Not surprisingly, he didn't last long as a church planter.

Financial abuse begins with a condition of the heart that has lost its perspective. Jesus said, "Watch out! Be on your guard against all kinds of greed; a man's life does not consist in the abundance of his possessions" (Luke 12:15). The reality is that church planting provides a fertile seedbed for greed. Why? The truth is that church planters are usually about as accountable as they want to be. Since there have been no preexisting boards (and in many cases, not preexisting agreed-upon procedures), church planters can quickly become freewheeling with the money entrusted to their ministries. And when boards do exist, church planters usually have enough power to influence decisions beyond what may be prudent. Contrast this with the writing of Peter to church leaders when he says, "Be shepherds of God's flock that is under your care, serving as overseers—not because you must, but because you are willing, as God wants you to be; not greedy for money, but eager to serve" (1 Peter 5:2).

Obviously there is protocol that must be implemented to guard against financial abuse. Having routine and accepted accounting (deposit and disbursement) procedures in order from the start is essential. But the important issue is the issue of the heart. The beauty of church planting is that there isn't anyone to tell us what to do; we have freedom. The pathology of church planting is that there isn't anyone to tell us what to do; we have freedom to become financial abusers! Church planters truly need to submit themselves to the Lord—guarding from every form of greed, including temptations such as:

"Opting out" of Social Security for financial purposes alone

Abusing other clergy tax advantages

Obsessively seeking clergy privileges and discounts

Blurring the line between a legitimate and illegitimate reimbursement

Using heavy-handed or guilt tactics for personal gain

Jeremiah spoke of spiritual leaders who went off track in the area of finances: "From the least to the greatest, all are greedy for gain; prophets and priests alike, all practice deceit" (Jeremiah 8:10). However, I do have a bit of encouragement for those who keep their hearts pure. While it is true that clergy are often underpaid, and while it is true the church planters often take more financial risk than other clergy do, the reality is that over time church planters

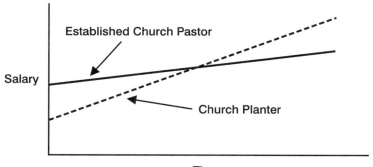

become some of the best-paid ministers, as described in this graph. Why is this often true? For one thing, the leaders and people of their church usually want to do everything they can to keep them around, so they tend to pay them well. My point is this: the temptation to abuse finances is real, but it's also true that, with patience, church planters tend to see themselves paid well — workers worthy of their hire.

I advise new church boards to pay their pastors well and take away their temptation to move along to greener pastures. Personally, I never turned down a raise, and I made efforts to teach my church to treat the pastor well. It's good to have earthly needs taken care of and to do well. Guiding the new church in that direction is a good thing, and it sets the church up well for the future, because the church won't have sticker shock when it comes to hiring its future pastors.

The basic scriptural admonition must be embraced: "Be shepherds of God's flock … not greedy for money, but eager to serve" (1 Peter 5:2). Take a quick glance at a biblical concordance and see how often the word "greed" is used in relationship to leaders. We must do what is necessary to thwart the evil one: set up accountability with your denominational leaders; invite scrutiny of the financial records; establish policies early; live above reproach.

2. The Abuse of Power

Some enter church planting for the very reason that they can have greater control. I can relate to that. When I heard someone say, "Why inherit someone else's problems when you can create your own?" I thought, "I'm in!" But the desire for freedom can subtly become a power trip. And Satan's temptation for power trips is legendary, even with regard to the temptation of Jesus. "Again, the devil took him to a very high mountain and showed him all the kingdoms of the world and their splendor. 'All this I will give you,' he said, 'if you will bow down and worship me.' Jesus said to him, 'Away from me, Satan! For it is written: "Worship the Lord your God, and serve him only" ' " (Matthew 4:8-10).

The abuse of power can be uniquely tied to church planting because a significant number of church planters are what as known as "high D" personalities. They function in the world of dominance, which, of itself, is not a bad thing. We need people who can push forward, control chaotic situations, and get the job done. As a matter of fact, a recent study among independent Christian churches found that strong dominant (or at least strong influence [or high "I"]) personalities were best suited for church planting success. Using the Personal Profile System, researchers surveyed 66 lead church planters, pairing their personality type with average worship attendance. Here's what they found:

High "D" (or Dominant) personalities averaged 181 after 5.2 years

High "I" (or Influencing) personalities averaged 174 after 3.6 years

High "S" (or Steady) personalities averaged 77 after 6.3 years

High "C" (or Compliant) personalities averaged 71 after 4.3 years

(*Source: The Orchard Group, http://www.gycm.org/Visionary/helps/mistakes.html.*)

Thus, high "D" and "I" personalities seem to win the day in terms of atten-dance as a success indicator—which only proves the point. Our strength is our pathology. Abuse of power lurks in the shadow of most successful planters. Sometimes dominance can get out of control, and even the church planter or the young church board can mistake control for leadership. Gary gave me a good word picture on this. It's of a strong-willed church planter leading the troops up the hill. He eventually gets to the top, but along the way the hill is littered with dead bodies. In the end, there is no one to enjoy the victory with.

Again, one part of the solution to the abuse of power is to voluntarily be placed under another authority — to have some accountability.

3. Pride

C. S. Lewis writes, "Pride is the last sin to die," meaning that it is founda-tional to every other sin. We place ourselves in the middle of a human-made universe where we make the rules and protect ourselves from external meddling. The opposite of pride is humility, where we see our lives in perspec-tive. The Apostle Paul writes, "For by the grace given me I say to every one of you: Do not think of yourself more highly than you ought, but rather think of yourself with sober judgment, in accordance with the measure of faith God has given you" (Romans 12:3). In what ways are church planters particularly vulner-able to pride? Here is a laundry list:

We think we're God's gift to the church.

We think we're relevant, and every other church or pastor is irrelevant.

We can't handle criticism of our model, our preaching, or our performance—even when we're wrong.

We name drop, or brag in other ways.

We're defensive and not open to coaching.

We avoid vulnerability and accountability.

Sure, anyone can be pride-filled. But church planters, who are often young, frustrated by-products of stagnant churches, can be exploited by the enemy in this corner of their lives. Pride needs to be checked. The Bible—and life itself—is replete with examples of those who lived inside an empty shell of self-worship and self-protection, only to lead to serious demise.

4. Illicit Sexual Relationships

No list of race-enders would be complete without a discussion of illicit sexual relationships. How are church planters uniquely vulnerable? Pastor and author Gordon McDonald, reflecting on his own adultery, put it this way: "An unchecked strength is a double weakness." In other words, if you're good at something, that something can easily be misused. The most obvious connection to church planting is that those who have the ability to start churches from scratch often have some other qualities that can be misused, such as attractive personalities, relationship-building gifts, capacity for empathy, and solid communication skills. Couple that with the fact that new churches exist to reach out to a hurting and needy world, and Satan has a pretty good opportunity to exploit us. The people we target to reach with the gospel come with enough baggage that, when joined with our own weaknesses, can lead to dangerous volatility.

Today it seems that the entry point for many leaders who are embroiled in illicit sexual relationships is pornography, especially from the internet. The statistics are not encouraging. Writes H. B. London, Vice President of Ministry Outreach/Pastoral Ministries for Focus on the Family,

> Sexual addiction is a major problem in the ministry. At Focus on the Family, we surmise that as many as one in five pastors have a problem in the area of pornography. Research in *The Sexual Man* shows that 15.5 percent of married men who are not clergy and 6.8 percent of married clergy continue to masturbate to pornography. Why? From his research, Dr. Hart concludes that sex has become dehumanized. In many circles, it is no longer regarded as an act between loving, responsible couples. Sex has become a sport. And, as in all sports, there is a strong desire to improve one's performance — pornography is a tool. Ministers are not excluded from this game.

(Source: *http://www.family.org/pastor/family/a0010907.cfm*. Accessed 12/15/04)

In the New Testament, James reminds his listeners of the progression of sin, warning that failure to bring a stop to harmful activity will eventually lead to destruction: " But each one is tempted when, by his own evil desire, he is dragged away and enticed. Then, after desire has conceived, it gives birth to sin; and sin, when it is fullgrown, gives birth to death" (James 1:14-15).

There is no silver bullet that I know of to slay this monster. It's fashionable to recommend some type of accountability group, but we must remember that accountability is only as good as we're willing to be honest. One district executive minister in my own denomination had a year where five ministers needed to resign because of adultery. Three of the five were in accountability groups. Understand what I'm saying: accountability is good. For instance, I am in an accountability relationship through Covenant Eyes (*www.covenanteyes.com*), so every place I visit on the Internet is reported to my partner. Accountability is helpful. However you should also take a ruthless inventory of your temptations in this area, communicate needs openly with your spouse, be open and honest about temptation, and devise a strategy that will keep you from being exploited.

5. The Neglect of our Physical Bodies

It's not surprising to hear people in ministry say, "I wish I had more hours in the day!" But some of those same people would never think to say, "I wish I had more years in my life!"

A good friend of mine, Dr. Sam Rima of Bethel Seminary, reminded me of this area. Sam has authored two excellent books about gaining victory over our leadership pathologies: *Overcoming the Dark Side of Leadership* (© 2000) and *Leading from the Inside Out* (© 2000). Sam and I were corresponding about the list of common race-enders; he wrote the following:

> Tom, one of the things I have always found curious by its absence from most lists is abuse of our physical body and our health. Though the Bible is silent on smoking and actually encourages the propitious use of wine, it has much to say about the care of our bodies and being good stewards of our physical health. Paul says we are to "glorify God with our body." There are numerous injunctions against gluttony, etc. I am convinced that many people are forced out of ministry prematurely by poor health as a result of failing to care for their body ... not body obsession, mind you, but body care. Things such as obesity, diabetes, hypertension, etc. all have a negative impact on longevity in ministry and finishing well. Without question, one of my most unhealthy periods was during my church planting days. Though I ran regularly, I was living at an unhealthy level of stress and eating poorly as a result, driven along by my compulsive and obsessive NEED to see my plant become a successful, growing church.

Sam is right. Even young and strong church planter can become cavalier about their bodies. I had a meal with a young church planter just last week who was mentioning his need to get his cholesterol under control—while munching down a large plate of onion rings.

6. Critical Family Issues

The Bible makes it clear that those in ministry who are single have an advantage over those who are married with families (1 Corinthians 7, for instance.) But most church planters are married and most have families, so this area becomes quite relevant. Some in ministry have become disqualified—or at least have been harmed deeply— because they neglected their families, and that neglect came back to bite them. While it's true that we don't have full control on how our spouses and children might respond to life (see the story of Samson, for instance), we do have responsibility to make sure that we do not sacrifice our families on the altar of ministry. Here, again, is a way in which the church planter becomes particularly vulnerable. Church planting is naturally a busy—sometimes frantic—pursuit. Unlike some established ministries that can function on auto-pilot for a while, church planting requires somebody to be working, or nothing gets done. So it's easy to neglect the family. It's almost laughable now, but I remember that on my first Labor Day in ministry I slipped into the office to do some computer work. It lasted all day long…on Labor Day! Hmmm…

When things go wrong in our families, every other aspect of our lives—including ministry—will suffer. Our response needs to be one of self-discipline, personal health, and spiritual vitality. And it does take discipline. I had one church planter ask me to hold him accountable for having a date night with his wife each week. I said, "Sure. I'll call your wife each week to see how it went!" He swallowed hard over that one, but he has maintained the discipline ever since.

7. Plateauing

Plateauing occurs when a person in ministry stops learning and growing, and as a result they settle into a pattern of doing what once worked with very little effort to expand. There is no great vision for the future, and there are no great attempts to get there. At first glance, this hardly seems like it should fit into a chapter on spiritual warfare. But this is not a chapter on spiritual warfare; it's a chapter on personal health and growth, and my caution would be to take care that plateauing doesn't dominate your life. In truth, most church planters are eager to learn. They become very pragmatic, and if something is working they usually want to be in on it. And most church planters don't envision the day when they will stop thinking strategically about the future. However this does happen.

One of my favorite visionaries is Steve Johnson, who has planted Community Church of Oshkosh, Wisconsin. Steve is one who embodies the opposite of plateauing. Steve used to tell the story of when he and Lynne planted a church in their early twenties. Nobody came to their first service. Nobody. However, eventually that church grew and planted a daughter church that has planted many other daughter churches.

That used to be a fun story for Steve to tell, but a few years back he decided to stop telling it. Why? He says, "I don't want to be known as one who took his greatest risk for God while he was in his twenties." Steve has also said to me, "Some of the greatest churches will never be planted…because those who are best equipped to do it will never take the risk again to do what they're uniquely qualified to do."

Enhancements

Let's counter with some ideas to enhance the possibility that we'll finish well. Again, the reminder is that life, like chess, is won or lost in the middle game. Sometime before age 55, and particularly between age 35 and 55, we need to be intentional about fighting the good fight. Here are some strategies that I've picked up from Dr. Bobby Clinton and others.

1. Intercessory Prayer Teams

In my discussion on spiritual warfare (see Chapter 8) I refer to individual and corporate prayer, and I make a foundation for its priority. I have made the following statement publicly many times, and I'm amazed at how people naturally nod their heads: "You'd be surprised how many people have no one who prays for them, and you might be surprised to know of how few people pray for you." That's rather sobering, considering that in our Christian subculture everybody endorses prayer. The idea of an intercessory prayer team is that you, as a Christian leader, are about the business of actively recruiting people to pray for you and you are in the habit of routinely communicating with them.

I've not considered myself a spiritual giant, but one thing I've done since day one in ministry is have a group of people pray for me. I'm talking about people who really pray. Most Christians will courteously agree to pray for you, even if they don't follow through. The key is to find people who really pray. How? Ask people if they know of people who really pray. Notice when people say, "I've been praying for you." And pray that God will bring you such intercessors.

I have about 20 intercessors on my team. They sign on until January 1 of each year, and then they can renew for that year. I get them a private prayer letter at least once a month, via email. They agree to try to pray for my ministry and my family each day. Some drop off at the end of the year, but most stay. And I'm constantly on the lookout for those who really do pray.

Having others who pray for you increases the likelihood that you'll win in the middle game and finish well. I once heard church growth expert Dr. Peter Wagner say modestly that his personal prayer habits were adequate but that his personal prayer life was outstanding—because he had others standing with him.

2. Disciplines: Ongoing Life of Spiritual Training vs. Trying

I stay in shape by running and lifting weights a few times each week. I usually run around four miles or so. Now what if for some reason I decided to run a marathon — 26.2 miles – today? Could I do it? Right now I'm not sure that I could. But suppose that you were alongside urging me to do it, and you kept saying, "Try harder! I know you can do it! Try harder!" Perhaps that could help, but if I'm really not in shape to run a marathon I still might fail.

On the other hand, what if you were my personal trainer and you said,

"Let's develop a plan to have you running a marathon within three months." Could I do it then? I don't see why not! It would be a matter of proper training and discipline. Lots of 46-year-olds run marathons. I probably couldn't do it if I simply "tried," but I could do it if I trained. Or, if I asked you to bench press 150 pounds, could you do it? If not, how about if you really, really tried? What if you tried harder? Well, if you couldn't bench press that amount to begin with, you probably couldn't do it by trying harder. But what if I said I could pair you with an Olympic caliber trainer, who would work with you over time to get you to the point of lifting that amount? Could that work? Probably.

Here's my point: when it comes to spiritual depth and power, training beats trying every time. After all, that's why we call them disciplines. Leaders who finish well typically have followed the rigors of spiritual training in areas such as prayer, fasting, solitude, and so on.

3. Renewal Times

The Bible prescribes renewal times for the children of God. There are admonitions to keep the Sabbath holy, and there are invitations to commemorative celebrations and festivals. Church planters and key leaders of church plants are not exempt from the need to find times of renewal in their lives. A few years ago I received a phone call from a church planter who had come upon some difficult times. Things weren't going well, despite the fact that he was working, working, working. I asked him to tell me about his last day off. He told me that he hadn't taken a day off in over a year, because the ministry was so busy. I pushed back on him, but he wouldn't budge. I asked, "What are you communicating to your people when you refuse to take time off?" He still wouldn't budge. I became so exhausted by the conversation that I finally said, "Fine. Live that way. Maybe you'll be the first church planter in history to plant a church in the power of the flesh!"

Times of renewal are what Steven Covey refers to as Quadrant 2 activities in his book *Seven Habits of Effective People* © 1990)They are non-urgent, but important. Personally, I have adopted the following template for finding times of renewal in my own life. I seek to:

Divert Daily, with a personal quiet time and Bible reading plan.

Withdraw Weekly, with a day off from ministry.

Maintain Monthly, with a retreat day.

Abandon Annually, with special events and extended vacations.

In our church planting movement, church planters sign a pledge to take at least one day off each week and to take at least one family vacation each year. For me, vacations give me a needed time of perspective. I'm the exact opposite of those who leave a vacation and say, "Well, now back to the real world." I say that when I leave home for a vacation: "Well, *now* back to the *real* world." In fact, I saw an advertisement in travel magazine for an enticing getaway that said, "It's not a vacation. It's practice for the afterlife!"

If church planters can't afford to take a vacation, we'll find a place and a funding source for them. It's just that critical. We also urge the taking of a monthly retreat day, which is not synonymous with a day off. It is a time for deeper reflection and gaining perspective. There are some excellent retreat materials available, including *A Guide to Ministers and Other Servants* (Shawchuck and Job, The Upper Room, 1983) that includes some specific monthly retreat models.

One other habit that we urge new churches to adopt is a sabbatical policy for pastoral staff. Generally speaking, the policy we recommend involves accruing 1½ days each month toward an extended sabbatical after five years of service. That equates to ninety days each five years. And one proviso of the policy is that pastoral staff who take a sabbatical must agree to continue on at the church for at least one year following the sabbatical, and not seek employment elsewhere. We find that this combination leads to healthy pastors having long pastorates — at healthy churches!

Renewal can come in other forms as well: a mission trip, conferences, a hobby, naps, whatever. The important thing is to remember that failure to be strategic and intentional for times of refreshment is a landmine we want to avoid.

4. Mentoring and Accountability

Those who finish well typically have had several key mentors over the course of their lives, people who have made an intentional investment to give general guidance and perspective. Bobby Clinton and Paul Stanley, in their excellent book, *Connecting: The Mentoring Relationships You Need to Succeed in Life*, © 1992, list three types of mentors: disciplers (who impart basics of the life of faith), spiritual guides (who focus on the mentoree's spiritual development and walk with God), and coaches (who address skill development). The authors also delineate between upward mentors (presumably older and more experienced) and peer mentors (comrades who can give "real time" perspective). We can also expose ourselves to historical mentors, whose writings leave a well of knowledge and inspiration for us. (One year, C. S. Lewis was my historical mentor. I took a book of his with me everywhere I went.)

My friend and colleague, Paul Johnson, makes a great analogy. He talks about a little girl who takes her first ice skating class, along with 29 other little girls. If she's good, she may take an advanced class, with nine other girls. If she's really good, she may be in an elite class with three other girls. And if she becomes so good, say to the point of being Olympic class, she will have several coaches: strength, nutrition, choreography, and so on. The lesson: the better athletes become, the more coaching they get. Shouldn't that be the same for ministry?

Accountability is a subset of mentoring. It's where we lay out our lives, weaknesses and all, to others so we may improve. Genuine accountability requires honesty, and that can only be generated internally. I mentioned above my accountability relationship on the Internet through a service called Covenant Eyes (*www.covenanteyes.com*), which reports to my partner. It's a freeing thing to be under accountability.

5. Being a Life-long Learner

The final enhancement that I'll discuss here is that of maintaining a learning posture. Life-long learners wage an attack against pride and plateau-ing. They are willing to believe that they don't have it all figured out and that they can learn from others. And they are unwilling to coast into the later years of life, running on fumes from years gone by. As I've said to some church planters, "Face it. In our twilight years we don't want to be stuck on the front porch of the Olde Church Planters' Rest Home, rocking in our chairs, mumbling about the direct mail piece we once sent out "that was *this* big"!

It's easy these days to be a lifelong learner. There are innumerable books, tapes, CDs, mp3 files, newsletters, Internet chat rooms, conferences, and so on available to us. There is no excuse to not be learning right up to the end.

A Concluding Word

I'll let friend and mentor, Dr. Greg Bourgond of Bethel Seminary in St. Paul, Minnesota, make a concluding comment as it pertains to those skilled young leaders who are doing the important work of planting new churches:

> Leadership competency may be the tools of effective leadership; but biblically informed character has always been the power of effective leadership. When a leader does not continually address character formation and transformation in their personal lives and operate solely from a competency base, then competency will ulti-mately fail to produce the kind of results God intended through the life of that leader.   And remember, lasting transformational change begins with the heart. Our central beliefs establish our core values, our values inform our worldview, our worldview conditions our primary motives, and our motives energize our behavior.   Our behavior merely reflects the condition of our hearts (Proverbs 4:23). The lesson: pay attention to the heart from God's point of view (1 Samuel 16:7), and God-honoring behavior will follow.

Questions to Ponder (While Standing in This Minefield)

How does the chess-game analogy apply to me?

Of the race-enders listed in this chapter, which one am I most vulnerable to? Who can I talk to about this? When?

Why do church planters so often compromise on their disciplines?

What is my plan to Divert Daily, Withdraw Weekly, Maintain Monthly, and Abandon Annually?

Whom will I pursue to mentor me?

How will I keep from plateauing?

LANDMINE 2:
LACK OF LEADERSHIP DEVELOPMENT

*You have heard me teach many things that have been confirmed
by many reliable witnesses. Teach these great truths to trustworthy
people who are able to pass them on to others.*
The Apostle Paul (2 Timothy 2:2 NLT)

*The key ability of winning organizations and winning leaders
is creating leaders.*
Noel Tichy

One of the landmines that church planters never dodge is the landmine of leadership development. I will never forget the day when I realized that there are no such things as "ready-made leaders." It was two years into our church plant with a boat full of converts and inexperienced leaders. I began hearing the same story over and over again from our leaders: very few of them had been personally mentored in the faith and in ministry.

Why was I shocked by this? I suppose it's because of my personal experience. It was only one month after I came to faith in Christ that I had a seasoned Christian mentoring me in my walk with Christ. Ray, a co-worker and former missionary in the jungles of Brazil, met with me every day for lunch for two and a half years. During that time I brought every question to him that you could imagine.

He imparted to me a love for Scripture and theology, and he introduced me to great historical leaders such as Jim Elliot, George Muller, David Brainerd, and George Whitefield. He helped me wrestle with my call to ministry. He gently challenged me, encouraged me, and inspired me to become all that God intended me to be. I can say that in those two and a half years God used Ray to lay a spiritual foundation in my life that has carried me for the last twenty-five years. Needless to say, I thought this was the normal experience for all believers. Everyone must have had a Ray in their lives!

But our church was lacking the leaders we needed to expand our ministry. Tom says that most church planters pray for God to bring them leaders, but God wants them to develop leaders on their own. How true that was for us. At that moment of realization I began to understand that there were four things that needed to be done. First, if we were going to grow as a church, I needed to champion leadership development as an essential characteristic of who we were as a church. In the book *Be-Know-Do: Leadership the Army Way* (Jossey-Bass, © 2004) the authors Frances Hesselbein and Gen. Eric K. Shinseki speak to the issue of how critical leadership development is to military life. They write,

> The American way of life and our well-being depend on the ability of Army leaders at all levels to inspire and lead, often under the most harrowing conditions and unimaginable levels of stress. And the Army has long understood that there is no substitute for strong leaders — throughout its ranks. During combat, squad leaders, platoon leaders, company commanders, and battalion commanders can be incapacitated or killed — as can their replacements and their subordinates. The cost of failure at any point in its complex formations could be catastrophic, as risks are most often measured in lives. Filling the ranks with well-trained, highly motivated, and performance-oriented soldiers who, without hesitation, can and will step forward to lead when victory hangs in the balance is the unrelenting requirement for success in battle. The Army, therefore, makes leadership everyone's priority. (p. xiv)

Second, I realized that we needed to make it a priority that every new convert and potential leader be provided an opportunity to be mentored in areas of spiritual formation, multiplication, and ministry leadership skills. Third, I realized that every leader is responsible not just to build a team and manage a task, but to spot, encourage, and develop other leaders under their care. Fourth, I realized that we needed a reproducible leadership development process that could expand with our growth and touch every level of this new work. Simply speaking, we needed a leadership culture.

Creating a Leadership Culture in a New Church

Every new church needs a leadership culture. And though it's easier said than done, it can be done. With intentionality, potential leaders can be spotted, trained, and deployed. No longer will you pray for God to bring you leaders, because leadership development will become normal and effective in your new church. Some simple but essential steps must be taken.

1. Develop a workable definition of what a leader is.

Many planters, in the early days, are anxious for leaders to be in place. After all, the work is a burden that needs to be shared. So they survey their young congregation and take their best shot. However, huge problems can result from the failure to discern the difference between spiritually mature leaders and naturally gifted leaders who are not spiritually mature. While we're glad for any natural or acquired skills that our people may have, having a church full of leaders without proper spiritual maturity can set off multiple landmines throughout the new church. We've all seen it: a leadership style that works in a business setting but is an utter failure in the business of leading the people of God. When this happens, the morale and spiritual temperature of a new church are compromised. J. Oswald Sanders, in his classic book *Spiritual Leadership* (Moody Press, © 1980), helps us see the difference:

NATURAL LEADERS	SPIRITUAL LEADERS
Self-confident	**Confident in God**
Know people	**Also know God**
Make their own decisions	**Seek to find God's will**
Ambitious	**Self-effacing**
Originate own methods	**Find and follow God's methods**
Enjoy commanding others	**Delight to obey God**
Motivated by personal considerations	**Motivated by love for God and people**
Independent	**God-dependent**

(*Spiritual Leadership*, p. 35)

We can give example after example of planters and lay leaders who, in the crucible of launching a new church, relied on their natural abilities to get the job done and in turn bruised and wounded the body of Christ. We have seen new churches go from 200 to 10 in six months because naturally gifted or educated laypeople were inappropriately empowered into positions of spiritual leadership. We have seen church planters drive away their launch teams by relying on their natural abilities to influence those around them. We have seen church planters lose their churches because of leadership backlash (which we address in the next chapter).

This is why we believe that a missing key to leadership development in the church is spiritual formation. Sanders writes, "Spiritual leadership is a matter of superior spiritual power, and that can never be self-generated. There is no such thing as a self-made spiritual leader. He is able to influence others spiritually only because the Spirit is able to work in and through him to a greater degree than in those whom he leads" (*Spiritual Leadership*, p. 33.) We will address the spiritual formation process later in this chapter.

Here are a few definitions of spiritual leadership to consider as you look to build a leadership culture in your new church.

> *"Spiritual leadership is moving people on to God's agenda"*
> Henry Blackaby & Richard Blackaby, *Spiritual Leadership*, (Broadman and Holman, © 2001) p. 20

> *"The central task of leadership is influencing God's people towards God's purposes"*
> Robert Clinton, *The Making of a Leader* (NavPress, © 1988) p. 203

> *"A Christian leader is someone who is called by God to lead; leads with and through Christ-like character; and demonstrates the function competencies that permit effective leadership to take place."*
> George Barna, *Leaders on Leadership* (Regal Books, © 1997) p. 25

> "Spiritual Leadership is knowing where God wants people to be and taking the initiative to get them there by God's means in reliance on God's power."
> John Piper, Brothers, *We Are Not Professionals* (Broadman and Holman, © 2002) p. 11

Having a good definition of spiritual leadership is critical to development of leadership cultural throughout your church. You need to know what you are shooting for if you are going to hit the target.

Embrace the "Apollos Principle"

As I mentioned above, new church leaders need to recognize that there is no such thing as a ready-made leader. Lynn Anderson, in his book *They Smell Like Sheep* (Howard, © 2002) offers the following insight,

> Shepherds do not come "one size fits all." "Elder" is not a generic category of a person who can transfer his leadership directly from this congregation to that. A good elder in one church may not begin to make a good elder in another. The Holy Spirit, through Paul the apostle, zip-coded his character sketches to specific churches. Apparently, God intended that each shepherd should fit his church situation. (p. 131)

Each church is a unique living organism, with its own DNA make-up, its own unique setting, its own mixture of personalities, and its own specific leadership needs. To think that a person who was an elder, small group leader, or ministry director in another church is automatically qualified to be one in your church is unfair to that person— and it can be dangerous for the new church. This is why we encourage church planters to embrace the "Apollos Principle"; every good leader — no matter how gifted or how used by God in the past — will be open to further instruction in order to make him or her into a more effective leader. This principle is named after Apollos, a great man of God. Luke gives us this description of him in the Book of Acts:

> Meanwhile a Jew named Apollos, a native of Alexandria, came to Ephesus. He was a learned man, with a thorough knowledge of the Scriptures. He had been instructed in the way of the Lord, and he spoke with great fervor and taught about Jesus accurately, though he knew only the baptism of John. He began to speak boldly in the synagogue. When Priscilla and Aquila heard him, they invited him to their home and explained to him the way of God more adequately. (Acts 18:24-26, NIV)

Apollos was a great man — well-educated, cultured, and eloquent. He knew God's Word, and he spoke with great passion and courage. And yet all the greatness didn't go to his head, because he was willing to receive more instruction from a couple of tent-makers. Great leaders are teachable leaders. In the end Apollos's usefulness to God's great cause expanded to the point that the Corinthian church began to look at him as equal to — or even superior to — the Apostle Paul (1 Corinthians 3:1-8).

Leaders who walk into your new church flashing their credentials of past experience but are unwilling to go through the normal assimilation process or leadership development system should be looked at with great suspicion and watched carefully. The Apostle Paul said to the elders in Ephesus, "Be shepherds of the church of God, which he bought with his own blood. I know that after I leave, savage wolves will come in among you and will not spare the flock. Even from your own number men will arise and distort the truth in order to draw away disciples after them. So be on your guard!" (Acts 20:28-31, NIV). And yet when an experienced leader comes humbly with a teachable spirit and wants to learn the church's unique vision, values, and personality, we need to work with them patiently and place them carefully into the life and mission of this developing community of faith.

Identify the emerging leaders in your midst

The next step in creating a leadership culture is to identify emerging leaders who should be developed. Three words help us navigate this process: pray, work, and look.

Pray. Jesus taught us that if we need leaders or workers we must first pray for them. "He told them, 'The harvest is plentiful, but the workers are few. Ask the Lord of the harvest, therefore, to send out workers into his harvest field'"

(Luke 10:2, NIV). Jesus not only taught his disciples to pray for leaders, he also modeled for them the need to pray for leaders. "One of those days Jesus went out to a mountainside to pray, and spent the night praying to God. When morning came, he called his disciples to him and chose twelve of them, whom he also designated apostles" (Luke 6:12-13, NIV). Again, we've seen enough church planters who keep scanning their flocks to find good leaders—but they've never sought God in this matter. How should we pray for leaders?

Pray for God to give you leaders out of the harvest for the harvest.

Pray for God to give you specific leadings in whom you should invest in as potential leaders.

Pray for God to give you fresh eyes to see the potential around you.

Work. If planters are going to identify leaders, they need to learn how to work their disciple-making or assimilation process well. If you work the system well and follow the modular training principle, you should uncover potential leaders in your midst. I work with a lot of churches that are implementing Rick Warren's purpose-driven baseball diamond approach. I am amazed at how many churches just let their people run the bases any way they want. This is what I call crazy baseball.

When I was a kid, my friends and I used to have fun by taking a baseball bat and holding it straight out in front of us. Then we would bend over, placing our foreheads on one end of the bat and the other on the ground, then begin running around it. After about five spins we would try to run the bases. The results were hilarious: most of the time we could not even stand up because we were spinning in all different directions. Even if someone pointed us toward first base, we would end up staggering toward third base.

In the purpose-driven model, the key place to find potential leaders is on third base. They have moved past discipleship and are now ready for ministry deployment. Leaders who work their disciple-making systems do, in fact, reproduce more leaders. No matter what your disciple-making process looks like — whether it is a baseball diamond, a business flow chart, a hiking map, or a funnel — we are convinced that if you fail to follow an intentional plan that you will naturally drift toward dependence on natural, rather than spiritual, leadership. The missing link in leadership development is a well-defined and well-executed spiritual formation process.

Look. Effective leaders are good spotters. They are on the lookout for potential leaders. They have the ability to look beyond other's deficiencies to see their possibilities.

Bob Logan gives the following advice for becoming a good spotter of potential leaders.

Look for evidence of giftedness in potential leaders; . . . the gifts may not yet be fully developed.

Look for character rather than social standing; . . . they may be a leader in the world, but that doesn't mean their character has been refined.

Look for faithfulness and humility rather than flashes of talent; . . . consistency to follow through with assignments (even when there is little recognition) demonstrates endurance.

Look for obedience rather than knowledge; . . . being faithful to do what they know is better than knowing a lot but never putting it into practice.

Look for willingness to learn rather than experience. . . . Someone who has "done it before" may not be willing to learn a new way of doing things.

Look for available people rather than the overworked leader; . . . too few leaders are carrying too much of the load. Find people who are ready for a new challenge.

(*www.Coachnet.org*. Accessed November, 2004)

4. Equip your leaders holistically

Today much of equipping leaders has to do with the skills of leadership, such as team building, recruiting, vision casting, and strategic planning. Yet, as we hinted earlier, we believe that the missing link in leadership development is spiritual formation, which leads to spiritual multiplication.

Why do we have board members who struggle in their prayer life? Why do you have people making critical decisions about the financial future of the church who don't worship God through their finances? Why do we have leaders who struggle with sharing their faith making decisions on the evangelistic strategy of the church? The answer to those questions is that we tend to empower those with natural leadership traits rather than those with spiritual leadership traits.

Here are the four areas that we feel are essential in developing spiritual leaders in your church.

Equipping them in the spiritual habits that are critical in their personal growth.

Training them in the areas of prayer, Bible study, worship, service, giving, building relationships with the unchurched, and sharing their faith story will be the focus in developing devoted disciples and potential leaders.

Equipping them in the formation of biblical values that will guide their thinking.

The number one struggle that converts wrestle with is embracing a biblical value system. Training them to think theologically and to be God-centered in their attitudes and in their decision making is vital to developing spiritual leadership in a new church.

Equipping them in the development of the essential life and ministry skills that will focus their giftedness and efforts.

Training leaders in the areas of financial stewardship and spiritual gifts discovery and development helps them focus their resources for the greatest impact. Equipping them in the areas of healthy relating, conflict management, team building, and coaching of others takes leaders to a new level as they begin to influence others toward the mission.

Equipping them in critical character traits that will ensure their effectiveness into the future.

Train leaders to take a rigorous spiritual inventory of their inner life – their desires, motives, and attitudes. Regularly exploring their behavior toward others and how their temperament and leadership style affect those around them are essential for the ongoing effectiveness and the deepening of their spiritual authority. Robert Clinton writes, "Spiritual authority is delegated by God and differs from authority that is based on position and force" (*The Making of a Leader*, NavPress, © 1988, p. 101). If spiritual authority is given by God, then it also can be removed by God. If leaders allow their inner life and relational life to fall into disrepair, they are in danger of losing all that God has bestowed on them.

5. Coach your leaders intentionally

The difference between coaching potential leaders and mentoring them can be traced to who initiates and sets the agenda. The coach says, "I am responsible, and I will be the initiator in our relationship." The mentor says, "I am available, and I will meet with you whenever you need me." What does the coaching relationship look like? It is relationship-intensive, filled with listening, caring, celebrating, and consistent encouraging. It is strategically challenging: asking good questions, thinking through critical issues, providing resources and ideas to go to the next level.

Connect

The coach take the initiative to *connect* regularly with the leader. Establishing trust and credibility is essential to the coaching relationship. Coaching involves coming alongside another as an ally and a partner to help identify leadership issues, process inner development, and determine the next steps to overcome the obstacles.

Clarify

The coach takes the initiative to *clarify* the leaders' progress toward their goals. This also includes reviewing progress, addressing obstacles, engaging in problem solving, and finding tools and resources that apply towards the goal.

Commit

The coach take the initiative to get the necessary *commitment* to a specific action plan. Each coaching session ends with concise action plans that help the leader, or leadership team to improve where desired. Creating the action plan is a joint effort between coach and leader with specific due dates for completion. Accountability makes the difference.

6. Celebrate your leader's achievements purposefully

Celebrating privately and publicly the achievements of leaders reinforces the work of God in their lives. It provides tangible examples to follow and reinforces the values of the new church. The Apostle Paul does this in his private letters to Timothy and Titus along with his public letters to Christians in Rome, Corinth, and Philippi. Paul writes to his young disciple Timothy, "Don't let anyone look down on you because you are young, but set an example for the believers in speech, in life, in love, in faith and in purity … Do not neglect your gift, which was given you through a prophetic message when the body of elders laid their hands on you" (1 Timothy 4:12, 14 NIV).

I can imagine this young leader saying, "God is not finished with me; I must stay the course in God's strength and complete the mission God has assigned me." Can you imagine the impact on Timothy's leadership development when he read these words that Paul wrote to the Christians in Philippi?

> I hope in the Lord Jesus to send Timothy to you soon, that I also may be cheered when I receive news about you. I have no one else like him, who takes a genuine interest in your welfare. For everyone looks out for his own interests, not those of Jesus Christ. But you know that Timothy has proved himself, because as a son with his father he has served with me in the work of the gospel. I hope, therefore, to send him as soon as I see how things go with me. (Philippians 2:19-23, NIV)

To praise and encourage upcoming spiritual leaders doesn't stoke their egos or give them a big head, as might some think, but instead humbles their spirit and drives them to rely more heavily on God — the true source of their power and effectiveness. Remember, these are spiritual leaders, and there is a real enemy accusing, attacking, and assaulting them from every angle. In all our years of ministry we have never met an over-encouraged lay leader, pastor, or church planter. However, we have met discouraged, unappreciated, and lonely leaders at all levels. Creating an atmosphere of ongoing encouragement keeps the young leader engaged emotionally, spiritually, and relationally. Sometimes that's the difference between a huge success and complete ineffectiveness.

Celebrating the accomplishments of young leaders publicly has a definite impact on the cultural of the new church. James Kouzes and Barry Posner, in their book *Encouraging the Heart* (Jossey-Bass, © 2003) write,

> When individuals or teams are singled out for recognition in a public event, they are held up as role models. Research shows that peers make better role models than those who are socially distant from us. Even if the president of a company were to behave consistently with our values, his would be an insufficient example. We need to see the behavior from the people like us. Public recognition offers leaders the chance to convey the message, "Here's some just like you. You can do this!" By awarding recognition in public to a person who represents the group, you not only give them much appreciated thanks but you also provide their colleagues with an example they can emulate." (pp.123-4)

Vince DiPaola, founding pastor of Lakeshore Community Church in Greece, New York, has embraced and practiced this principle since the early days of his church plant. In their quarterly newsletter, *Real Encouragement*, they have a section called *"Giant Killers"* to celebrate the achievements of the up-and-coming leaders in their church. Here is an example:

Jim & Sue Strowe: October 2004 Giant Killers

Meet the Strowe family — Jim, Sue and Will — all dedicated Lakeshore Community Church members. This remarkable family has called Lakeshore their home since 2003. One quality that many have come to love and appreciate about the Strowes is their love for serving others.

Sue serves on the Global Impact Team, the CARE team, and the FriendShip Company, where she enjoys making a difference in the lives of those with whom she interacts. Her husband, Jim, is credited with establishing the LCC parking ministry. Their son, Will, is also a valuable member of the parking team, as well as being the youngest traffic specialist.

When the new facility opened, Jim noticed that parking could potentially be a problem. In effort to circumvent this situation, Jim thought it would be a great idea to have a team in the parking lots to direct traffic; especially with the addition of a 2nd Sunday service.

Jim says that the parking team is a "logical extension" of the greet team, where friendly faces direct LCC members and guests to create a pleasant parking experience.

Look for the Strowe family at Lakeshore. They have embodied the church's mission with their initiative and commitment to serving others. Next time you pull into the parking lot, be sure to say hello!

If you are going to create a culture that raises up new leaders, then make sure that celebration happens!

7. Multiply by starting with the mind of the leader

If leadership development is going to be a priority for a new church, then it is critical to develop a multiplying mindset through every level of the church. In the U.S. Army's leadership training manual there is a wonderful description of a culture of leadership development:

"At any level, anyone responsible for supervising people or accomplishing a mission that involves other people is a leader. Anyone who influences others, motivating them to action or influencing their thinking or decision making is a leader. It's not a function only of position; it is a function of role. In addition, everyone in the Army – including every leader – fits somewhere in the chain of command. Everyone in the Army is also a follower or subordinate. There are, obviously, many leaders in an organization, and it's important to understand that you just don't lead subordinates – you lead other leaders. Even at the lowest level, you are a leader of leaders." (*Be, Know, Do*, Jossey-Bass, © 2004, p. 6)

Every leader in your church must see that they are not just leading a small group but are leading a group of potential small group leaders. Those who lead your ushers or greeter teams must move beyond getting the task done to seeing themselves doing on-the-job training for future leaders. Your pastoral staff must move beyond filling leadership slots to raising up pastoral leaders and missionaries for the harvest field.

When we think of developing a leadership culture in a church, our minds run to Joseph, a Levite from Cyprus who earned from the rest of the apostles the nickname of Barnabas, "the son of encouragement." His story is found throughout the book of Acts. Barnabas accepted an assignment to work with the new church that was forming in Antioch. There he joined the wonderful work that God was doing throughout that city. The people followed his leadership, and with his generous spirit, positive outlook, and strong spiritual example, he moved this new church from being a place overrun with converts into a church that touched the known world of his day.

As John Piper describes him, Barnabas was a "leader maker." God used Barnabas's gifts to create a culture within the church in Antioch that gave a chance to a leader who had apparently been sidelined in Tarsus. After he arrived in Antioch, for a full year this new leader, Paul, worked together with Barnabas, teaching large numbers of disciples. Then, one day God spoke to Barnabas and Paul about taking a fresh ministry assignment to influence the known world. There could have been no Apostle Paul without Barnabas, the leader maker.

A reading of Acts 15 reminds us that these men knew each other and labored together for fifteen years, until a sharp disagreement arose between them. From that point on, they ceased working together. We find it very interesting that this sharp disagreement was over another young would-be leader, who was apparently sitting on the sidelines looking for another opportunity — John Mark, the author of the Gospel that bears his name. Whichever way you look at it, the development of young leaders was so critical in the mission of the early church that good men struggled to come to agreement over how to handle it. When we value leadership development in the same way, we're avoiding another critical landmine in the planting of our churches.

Questions to Ponder (While Standing in This Minefield)

How do my personal insecurities cause me to seek the wrong leaders?

Where have I seen the Apollos Principle violated? What were the results?

Who are three potential leaders that I need to approach? What will be my plan to develop them?

How can I become more intentional in my coaching? Where can I be taking the initiative?

How can I hold leaders accountable?

In what ways will I encourage leaders, both publicly and in private?

LANDMINE 3:

LEADERSHIP BACKLASH

Honest criticism is hard to take, particularly from a relative,
a friend, an acquaintance, or a stranger.
Franklin P. Jones

The key to being a good manager is keeping the people who hate me
away from those who are still undecided.
Casey Stengel

One of the reasons I got into church planting to begin with was something I heard Bob Logan say when I was a student at Denver Seminary. He asked, "Why would you want to inherit someone else's problems when you can create your own?" That resonated with me. Leading an established church seemed so messy to me. I had seen good pastors get beat up too much, fighting with preexisting leadership boards. You've already read about my friend in the 115-year-old church that had stacks of picture frames ready for the next employee-pastor (see Chapter 1). I didn't like the idea of being an employee.

So I thought I'd start a church, in part because I didn't want the hassle of dealing with leadership that was there before I was. I didn't want to inherit someone else's problems; I wanted to create my own! In truth, my years as founding pastor of Community Church in Whitewater, Wisconsin went pretty well. I don't recall any significant stare-downs with my leadership teams. (One guy with issues accused me of having issues, but that wasn't really too bad.) However, I have learned something over the years that brings us to this chapter. Even in new church plants we shouldn't be surprised to encounter significant seasons of leadership backlash.

What is leadership backlash? I define it as " a surprising and antagonistic reaction from other church leaders to a trend, development, or event that you hold closely." Dictionaries call backlash "a sudden or violent backward whipping motion", and that comes pretty close to it in church life! There are thousands of examples of leadership backlash in the church planting Hall of Fame. Common battle grounds include:

Philosophy of ministry

Degrees of seeker sensitivity

Role of women

Advertising and marketing

Missions philosophy

Birthing a daughter church

Home schooling

Having a Christian school

Purchasing land

Constructing a building

Incurring debt

Polity and leadership structure

Preaching

Church planter David Howie of Lake Geneva, Wisconsin, put it this way, "I have spent six months tattooing our vision and values on their foreheads! But they are not tattooed on their hearts until your vision and values are challenged and tested." Wise church planters and new church leaders will do well to know that these things come. The Apostle Peter gave similar advice to church members who found themselves in the midst of the battle: "Dear friends, do not be surprised at the painful trial you are suffering, as though something strange were happening to you" (1 Peter 4:12).

I'm not suggesting that you take a posture of paranoia, but please realize that things are not always as they seem. I saw a cartoon of a dentist peering into the mouth of a patient as he says, "You might feel a little tingle. On the other hand, you might feel like you've been kicked in the mouth by a mule!" So it's good to prepare should leadership backlash come. You should not consider it strange. The Bible is full of leadership backlash stories, as is all of church history. Scott Arbeiter, Senior Associate Pastor at Elmbrook Church in Milwaukee, Wisconsin wisely told me, "You will visit these seasons, but you don't want to live in them. Be careful not to get locked into a deal you can't live with."

The Role of Value and Agenda Disharmony

The basic difficulty that occurs is one of **value and agenda disharmony**. In other words, as time goes on, the leadership team discovers that they are at odds with one another over certain issues affecting the direction of the church. This is not unlike a marriage, where partners thought they knew what the other person was like, but now are finding a completely different picture. But unlike marriage, where the partners are committed to working things through because of their pledge to stick together for better or worse, leadership teams in new churches operate on an entirely different set of assumptions.

Gary tells a humorous story of discovering something surprising about his father—a hidden agenda item that came to light this past year. Nearly everyone who grows up in Wisconsin becomes a Green Bay Packers fan, Gary included. This past year his father invited him to a Packers vs. Dallas Cowboys game at Lambeau Field in Green Bay. When Gary got to his seat, he was shocked to see his dad dressed in full Cowboys gear. He had been a closet Cowboys fan for years, and this game was his "coming out" party!

Even those closest to you may have some surprising values and agenda disharmony issues! When care has not been exercised in choosing an initial leadership team, and wrong assumptions have been made relative to the purpose and tenure of that initial leadership team, the result is painful for everyone. Following are some of the causes for such problems:

There have been pre-existing leaders, who may have been on site prior to the arrival of the church planter. These leaders have had the initial vision for the new church, and they have already been making decisions about the new church. It is natural (though not necessarily healthy) for them to assume that they will be the future leaders of the church. They expect the church planter to follow their terms. When it is discovered that "we're not on the same page", tensions mount.

There are often insecurities on behalf of the church planter. The planter may be new to pastoral ministry, can be intimidated by stronger personalities, and would not want to risk hurting someone's feelings by not inviting them to join the team. They want everyone to be happy, but as we'll see, long-term harmony is often sacrificed for short-term peace.

The planter has limited time available, especially if bi-vocational and fails to exercise care in choosing leaders. And, frankly, planters are happy that at least someone wants to serve and take some of the leadership burden away.

Potential leaders feel pressure to serve. In their heart they know that this is not their role, but the planter needs help, so they decide to serve in a leadership role. It would be in their best interest and in the best interest of the church if they were to serve in another capacity.

Some potential leaders were not allowed to lead in previous church. experiences, so this is their opportunity to be a key influencer. No one, including planters/pastors, has entirely pure motives, but on some occasions there are those whose motives are blatantly impure.

Assumptions are made that the initial leaders will be perpetual leaders. When disharmony or other issues arise, it is only with great pain that leaders are asked or forced to leave the team. There is no clean way to leave a leadership team or to remove someone from a leadership team.

Diagnose First, and Keep Diagnosing

To better understand whom to place in leadership and whom to avoid, let's start with a solid understanding of values. Values are those deeply held beliefs that become non-negotiables, and they are the cradle of problems. When my values differ from yours, it's likely that we will have some sort of friction. And our best bet when working together is to know as much about each others' values up front.

Management writer and consultant Ken Blanchard recommends that the primary leader of the organization (in this case, the church planter) list and rank his or her own values, with the non-negotiables right at the top. Remember, past behavior is the best indicator of who we really are and what we'll be, so think of values in terms of your history more than in terms of your preferences. Chuck Smith was the founder of the Calvary Chapel movement. Once they constructed a building in their Costa Mesa, California, location some of the church leaders started complaining that barefoot church attendees were soiling the carpet. Chuck reportedly, left the board meeting and came back a few minutes later with tools that he used to start tearing up the carpet! If the leaders didn't already know it, they knew it right then and there that Chuck Smith valued lost people more than carpet.

Church planters should get their non-negotiables out there for others to see. *The Church Planters' Toolkit* (ChurchSmart Resources, © 1991)offers some "values and agenda harmony" worksheets that can get you on your way. These same sheets can also be distributed to potential leaders for them to articulate their own values and compare them to the church planter's. One way or another, the church planter needs to remember "the power of paper" and get his or her values in print, as a values gauge with other leaders. And remember that vision disagreements ("how we accomplish our mission") rarely hurt churches, but values disagreements can be fatal.

Another friend, church planter and coach Dave Mobley (Woodridge Community Church, Milwaukee), helped me think of values and agenda issues in terms of a matrix. I think this can be very helpful, so take a few minutes to

How do they feel about you personally?

		OK	Not Sure
How do they feel about your vision and values?	**OK**	**Quadrant 1:** Work with these people; they believe in you and the mission. Monitor for signs of erosion.	**Quadrant 2:** Spend time with these people; looking for ways to build your relationship.
	Not Sure	**Quadrant 3:** Look for ways to inform and educate these people. Give them opportunities to see the model in action.	**Quadrant 4:** Short-term missionaries at best. Be up front about your differences, and perhaps outcounsel them to other churches.

study this diagram and consider where leaders and prospective leaders in your church line up.

I want you to understand this matrix, because shortly I'll add some things that will be even more helpful. We basically have four types of people who are potential leaders in your church. Quadrant 1 people believe in you personally, and they believe where you're taking this church. These are your key leaders, so thank God for them and work with them. As a wise leader of leaders you'll also monitor how things are going so you can avoid their slipping into quadrants 2 or 3.

Quadrant 2 refers to those who like your model, but they aren't sure that they like you personally or that they believe in your competency. Say, for example, that you were planting a Saddleback "purpose-driven" church model. Imagine that a potential leader in your new church actually came from Saddleback Church in Southern California, and she knew the model inside and out. But, by the same token she also knew and loved Rick Warren, Saddleback's pastor. She quickly has discovered that you're not Rick Warren, and you're not quite the pastor that he was. She's in quadrant 2. As you relate to such people and demonstrate your competencies, you have a chance to win them into quadrant 1. However, you might also disappoint these folks, and they could end up slipping into quadrant 4.

Quadrant 3 speaks of those who already know and like you, and they probably appreciate your competencies. The only problem is that they don't believe in the model of church you're espousing. This can happen when there is a parent church that has supplied some of your core group people. The people join the new church because they already know and believe in the pastor. But they also learn that their pastor friend doesn't plan to do church the same way as it was done in the parent church. These people need to be educated and informed so they can be moved into quadrant 1.

Let's say the new model is a Willow Creek "seeker-driven" model. Why not take these people to visit a seeker-driven church, interview some of the leaders there, and help to inform and educate them? Most won't embrace the model right away, but when they see it actually work in your setting they will probably join quadrant 1. When I planted a church, one core group member was in quadrant 3. He couldn't believe that we would spend so much money on direct mail to advertise the opening of the church. But when he saw it work, he became the champion of direct mail throughout the years that I was there. Remember, if quadrant 3 people don't buy in, they will slip into quadrant 4.

Quadrant 4 speaks for itself. These people either have never believed in you and your mission, or they slipped there from either quadrant 2 or 3. Once there, it's hard to get them to backtrack, and in most cases you wouldn't want them back. You can broker "short-term missionary" deals, where they could agree to serve for a specified time to help get you off the ground. If you do that, be clear about expectations and don't over-empower them. Another option is to respectfully and firmly outcounsel them to other churches that would be in line with their vision and values.

Look at the new version of the diagram. It's the same as the other one, but I've added a few things to illustrate some points. First of all, notice the block arrows. They show that people don't naturally move from quadrant 1 to quadrant 4. They always go through quadrants 2 or 3 first.

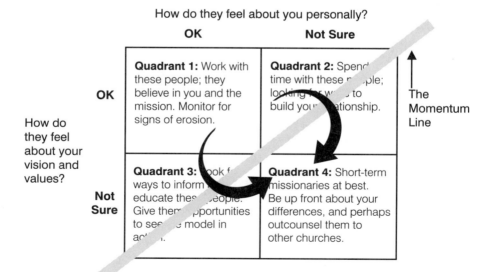

The implication here is that quadrants 2 and 3 are tricky: they're temporary holding chambers. People don't stay in quadrant 2 forever. They either start liking and believing in you (and move to quadrant 1), or they jump down to quadrant 4 and move on. Nor do people stay in quadrant 3 forever. They either start believing in the model and move to quadrant 1, or they abandon you and the model and head for quadrant 4 and move on.

This brings us to the big block diagonal line that I call "the momentum line." Why? After looking at church planters and the landmine of leadership backlash throughout the years, I believe that momentum is the key to determining which way people go. Think of the momentum line as a "continental divide" that pushes people one way or another. Positive momentum pushes quadrant 2 and 3 people into quadrant 1. And negative or a lack of momentum pushes quadrant 2 and 3 people into quadrant 4.

Let's say that the church plant goes well. People are won to Christ, they are assimilated into the church and their lives are changed. Even though you're not Rick Warren, the Saddleback folks will jump from quadrant 2 to 1. And the guy who became our direct mail champion? Well, the reason he moved to quadrant 1 was because he saw so much momentum. He thought, "Who am I to argue with what God is blessing?"

A Solution that Works

My advice to church planters, then, is to get a good handle on aspiring leaders and see what you can do to pray and move them into quadrant 1. They like you and believe in you. Good. But some will slip into quadrant 2 or 3 and maybe even 4 over time. So how do you raise up leaders for your formal leadership board without running into huge agenda and values conflicts? The solution is based on at least four principles:

1) Multiple leadership phases must occur before a formal

   board is chosen.

2) Church-sounding nomenclature must be avoided

   as these leadership teams are formed.

3) Titles which imply permanence (such as "board") must be avoided

   during these developmental phases.

4) A clear purpose and time-frame for each phase must exist.

5) A changing of the guard must occur at each phase.

Here's how this comes together. Suppose the church planter is on site with an emerging core group or launch team. Perhaps there are thirty adults now, offerings are being received, and there is a need for a leadership team to be formed. The major mistake a church planter could make at this point is to appoint elders. That would be, in my opinion, a violation of Paul's instruction to Timothy (1 Timothy 5:22). Rather, the planter should adhere to the above principles and follow a plan similar to the following.

Phase 1: The Pastor's Advisory Team

The first thing to do is call together a group of people whose purpose is to help the church planter make significant decisions while this church is growing its team and preparing to launch public services. Participants are told clearly (in writing) that they are being invited to help the planter make important leadership decisions *up until the time the church is launched publicly*. After the church is public, the Pastor's Advisory Team will be dissolved, and a new team will rise up to take its place.

Phase 2: The Transitional Advisory Group ("TAG Team")

After the church is launched, the Pastor's Advisory Team (PAT) meets one more time to celebrate the victory. The planter reminds them that the PAT is now dissolved. Over the next few weeks he or she will prayerfully consider formulating a new leadership team to take the church to the next level. Some from the PAT will be invited to participate, but others will step aside and make room for newcomers.

Yes, this is a benevolent dictatorship. Yes, some people will want to stay who shouldn't, and there is the possibility of some misunderstanding. But it is much better than any other alternative. The planter will then prayerfully decide who should stay, who should step aside, and which newcomers should be invited to participate in the Transitional Advisory Group, or TAG Team. A letter will be sent specifying that the purpose of the TAG Team is to help the planter make important leadership decisions, for instance, *during the first year of the new church's life*. After the first anniversary the TAG Team will be dissolved, and a new team will rise up to take its place.

Phase 3: The Short-term Leadership Team

After the first anniversary of the new church, the TAG Team meets one more time to celebrate the victory. The planter reminds them that the TAG Team is now dissolved. Over the next few weeks he or she will prayerfully consider formulating a new leadership team to take the church to the next level. Some from the TAG Team will be invited to participate, but others will step aside and make room for newcomers.

Yes, this is still a benevolent dictatorship. Yes, again, some people will want to stay who shouldn't, and there is the possibility of some misunderstanding. But it is much better than any alternative. The planter will then prayerfully decide who should stay, who should step aside, and which newcomers should be invited to participate in the Short-term Leadership Team. Again, a letter will go out, specifying that the purpose of the SLT is to help the planter make important leadership decisions, for instance, until there is a self-governing church that is operating under its constitution. After that, the SLT will be dissolved, and the church will start to operate according to its constitution's leadership structure.

Phase 4: The Formal Board/Elders/And so forth

By this time, enough water has gone under the bridge for the planter and the leaders of the church to have a pretty good idea of who should work with whom, and who might be best suited for formal leadership roles with a longer commitment. Many of the value and agenda harmony issues have now been resolved, and a number of other benefits have been achieved—not the least of which is that the church has started to model that leaders come and go, and that no one is indispensable.

Further Recommendations

Use whatever names you want, and as many phases as you need. The above four- phase scenario is just a suggestion. You may find that you need more or fewer phases. But be sure to steer clear of names such as *elder, deacon, overseer* during these early phases, and stay away from titles that imply permanence.

In the beginning, don't give away roles, give away jobs. This is very important in the early days of a church. *Roles* connotes titles, position, and policy making, but *jobs* connotes service. Once a "role" is given away, it can be difficult to take it back if necessary. Until you are absolutely sure of a person's match for a role, don't assign it.

Hold onto your principles tightly, hold onto your personnel loosely. In the long run, the mission will be better served when sound principles and procedures are followed, rather than subjugating these principles to accommodate people. It is normal in church life for people (including leaders) to come and go, and we are wise to hold them loosely.

In the beginning, not all leaders need to come from the church you're planting. That's right, often you can find others to join your team who come from another church—perhaps a trusted quadrant 1 friend— who has some experience and can give objective perspective to the emerging church.

Choose short-term pain and long-term gain. If there are leaders who want to be part of the next phase but aren't being invited, tell them "I'd rather have you dislike me in the short run and like me in the long run than the other way around."

Sure, you'll still have hassles. But you'll be much better off than if you were haphazard in your approach to developing your leadership team.

Some have suggested that the church planter should have to defend his or her choices to their coach or supervisors. This would both serve as a screening process and take some of the pressure off the church planter when it comes to inter-church politics.

Benefits of the Multiphase Approach

In the first days of a church some early adopters will join with great vision and enthusiasm but sometimes without perseverance, leadership skills or proven character. They can be very helpful as interim leaders. However, many will not move on to the next leadership phase. Utilizing multiple leadership phases helps move them out of leadership into another area of service.

The second leadership phase, the TAG Team, then enables the church planter to add some late adopters to the team while moving other leaders to another task. Also, during the first year the launch team will be expanding, so having a second stage allows the freedom and flexibility to add new leaders who have come on board since the first leadership phase.

The third phase, or the "Short-term Leadership Team", allows the planter to further observe potential leaders, add new leaders, and ease out some leaders. This is a good time to add some "specialists" to the team: people with skills and interests in writing, theology, documentation, organization, and so on. It is during this phase that the Constitution, Statement of Faith, and formal leadership structure is often clearly defined.

General benefits to following this approach include modeling flexibility in leadership, modeling leadership as service, providing greater flexibility in identifying and slotting leaders, ease of assimilating and incorporating new leaders (keeping "power brokers" to a minimum), freedom to involve godly and gifted women without a great deal of theological struggle, and time to prayerfully discern God's leadership choices.

Scott Arbeiter gave me a great word picture that sums up this strategy. Church leadership phases can be likened to a relay race on a track. Each phase of the race is vital, and each is dependent upon the others. However, imagine the absurdity of one runner refusing to hand the baton off to the next runner when the time came. If that would happen the entire team might lose. As Scott says, "Leaders need to understand the beauty of mutual submission, and when it comes down to it, it's all about the growth of God's Kingdom and not about our individual agendas."

Maintenance for the Long Haul

Following the above approach will make a big difference in shrinking the landmine of leadership backlash. However, as in any human relationship, there is the possibility of slippage over time. Genuine and sincere values and agenda discord can occur, even among leadership boards who have been shoulder to shoulder for many years. Gary recommends an annual checkup with your leaders by using the following four questions:

Who am I? What is my role on this team? What is God calling me to?

Who are we? As an organization, what is our unique calling?

Where are we going? What is our primary destination? What should result?

How are we going to get there? What specific methods and processes will we employ?

It's a mini-version of a "values and agenda harmony" survey, and it can be easily administered in the context of a leadership meeting or a retreat. Leaders can fill out the survey ahead of time, limiting their answers to a specified length. The idea is to get values and agenda issues out on the table before there is significant conflict. To be sure, any team of leaders will at one time or another find some differences of opinion. That is to be expected and welcomed. But when values and agenda disharmony runs deep, it must be diagnosed early. The only way to ensure that is to have regular checkups. When these are done on a routine basis, the landmine of leadership backlash will certainly be softened and possibly even avoided.

Questions to Ponder (While Standing in This Minefield)

When have I made incorrect assumptions about others' values and agendas that have resulted in backlash?

Do I have the courage to accept short-term pain over long-term pain?

Who are my quadrant 2 and quadrant 3 people? What is my plan to help move them toward quadrant 1?

How will we create momentum? How will we pray?

Are there other trustworthy leaders from outside our church that could serve for a season?

How will we regularly diagnose our leaders' value and agenda harmony issues?

LANDMINE 4:

PERSONAL EVANGELISM ENTROPY

He who conquers others is strong; he who conquers himself is mighty.
Lao-tzu

When interviewing church planting candidates, I frequently ask, "Why do you want to start a new church?" The response, though articulated in different ways, always has something to do with reaching the unchurched or the next generation for Christ: "I want to start a church that effectively reaches lost people" or "I want to impact my generation that has given up on church." We see this motivation expressed in the vision statements of their new churches:

> Bringing people together in a relationship with God – from Rogers Park, to Chicago, to the world.

> To glorify God by helping people find and follow God.

> Turning nonbelievers in our community and worldwide into fully developing Christ followers with lives of significance and fulfillment through the work of the Holy Spirit.

Evangelism is always on the front burner when a leader is considering or planning to start a new church. But even the most well-intentioned church planters can lose focus and find themselves right in the middle of another landmine—one that we call evangelism entropy.

"Entropy is the natural and irreversible tendency toward disorder in any system without an external source of energy" (*The Wordsmyth English Dictionary*). When we apply this principle to evangelism, we need to recognize the fact that, left to itself, the energy of evangelism in the local church will naturally (and in some cases irreversibly) move toward disorder. Bruce McNichol cites a well-known statistic: "A church which is 0 to 3 years old takes 3 attendees to reach one person for Christ. A church which is 3 to 10 years old takes 7 attendees to reach one person for Christ. A church older than 10 years takes 89 attendees to reach one person for Christ." Bill Hull writes, "The average church in America today sees 1.0 adult conversion per year, per one hundred in attendance. This might be expected of former mainline — now sidelined – churches, but it is a surprise that evangelicals do only a tad better, with 1.7 per one hundred in attendance" (Revival that Reforms, Fleming Revell, © 1998, p. 41) As the church gets older and older, it becomes harder to keep evangelism on the front burner because of all the competing issues that keep pushing it back.

To successfully navigate the entropy of evangelism in a new church, you must first understand the three spheres of evangelism that each church planter encounters as well as the general solution to reaching these people:

People who know you and your church. (The solution: modeling)

People who know your people. (The solution: equipping)

People who don't know you, your people, or your church. (The solution: marketing)

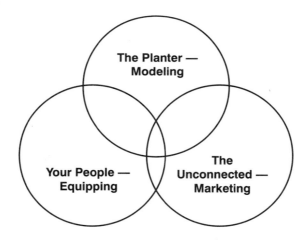

The first sphere church planters need to embrace is that of their own personal contacts. When church planters move into a community, it is amazing how many contacts they and their families generate. The stories we hear of neighbors, insurance agents, and community leaders coming to know Christ within months of the church planter moving into the area are thrilling. Why does that slow down as the church gets older?

Let us examine a few issues. The first one is the abdication of responsibility by the church planters themselves. Why would some whose chief motivation was to reach people quickly resign themselves from evangelistic activities? Here are two common reasons: burnout and balance. Pioneer church planters, those without a "running start" with a core group, are fully engaged in evangelistic activities out of the sheer need for survival. The ability to network in the community and to engage it evangelistically rests solely on their shoulders, and the burden of that responsibility is intense. The constant load of rejection they encounter can lead to burnout. One of my church planters said, "If you really want to gain a little understanding on the condition of the church in America, just drop yourself into a community not knowing a soul. Every time I shared my vision with churched people, they looked at me as though I was an alien from another planet." The face of that constant rejection can be very demoralizing.

Another factor that can lead to burnout is the lonely nature of the job, especially for those who come out of thriving ministries. The shock of going to a community where nobody really cares that you are there can be debilitating. I usually try to prepare pioneer church planters with a little pep talk like, "When you get into town, you need to push yourself to meet people because the only people who care that you are there will be me and Jesus!" That is an overstatement. I am sure that there are many people who care that they are there. The only problem is that none of them live in that town. This is why it is so important for a church planting coach to call the church planters at least once a week and meet with them once a month. Coaches need to help their planters achieve the resolve necessary to move forward.

The final factor for burnout is the intense care of new believers. Converts come in all sizes and shapes, with all sorts of baggage. They have messed-up marriages, damaged emotional lives, self-centered values, screwed-up finances, and whacked-out priorities. They have no knowledge of God, the Bible, or the church. Seeing them through these issues with proper follow-up and discipleship can be a very draining and frustrating experience.

I remember a time when I cried out to God. It was eighteen months after we had started a new church. I was working a couple of jobs. We had grown from 2 families to about 40 families, of which about 80 to 90 percent were people who weren't believers yet, had just trusted Christ, or had just started coming back to Christ. I remember yelling at God, saying, "If you don't bring me any help in the next six months, I am going to quit!"

Did it mean that I didn't love lost people? No! I just revealed that I was burned out. John Maxwell has said, "There's no such thing as burnout. It's just people who are taking themselves too seriously." In principle I believe that. But when you're on the front lines and ministry is such a struggle, you seriously do need some tangible help. Within two weeks of my crying out, God provided two spiritually mature couples who partnered with me in establishing the church. One of those leaders is still an elder in that church today.

Balance is another reason why church planters abdicate their evangelistic responsibilities. We commonly see this with those who come out of a strong parent church. It is not unrealistic for this type of planter to have a hundred churched contacts to follow up. Although the mission statement said something about reaching unchurched people, the truth is that churched people take time. A church planter's time can get swallowed up just recruiting the already convinced. If church planters are not disciplined in networking and spending time with unchurched people, they can end up starting a church for the churched instead of a church to reach the community. We recommend that our church planters spend at least 50 percent of their work week in networking and developing pre-Christian contacts.

Here are a few simple de-mining techniques to help you negotiate this landmine of evangelism entropy.

1. Remember that you are a missionary to your community.

In our training program we give five ways for planters to enter a new community. First, they need to enter it as an intercessor, praying for the community at large. Second, they need to enter as a learner, grasping the historical, cultural, and social dynamics of their community. Third, they need to enter it as a servant, finding ways to be involved in community life that reflect the heart of a servant. One of my church planters went to the mayor of his town and asked where he could serve. The mayor was flabbergasted and said, "You are the first pastor ever to come ask how you could serve the community." Fourth, they need to enter it as a friend or an ally, strategically and intentionally building friendships throughout the community. Finally, they need to enter it as a storyteller, continuously sharing the gospel and the vision for the new church. If church planters are going to seriously deal with evangelism entropy within their own lives, they need go back to the basics of why they came at all. Here are a series of questions one should prayerfully reflect upon:

How am I intentionally and strategically praying for my community?

What am I learning about my community's history, social structures, and future?

How do the community leaders know that I am here to serve and not just to be served?

What strategic friendships and partnerships am I building?

How many times a week am I sharing the gospel, getting into spiritual discussions, and sharing the vision for a new church?

2. Upgrade your networking skills.

Ray Bakke writes, "Pastors who network their communities, especially in the first year of a pastorate, may end up knowing that community better than any other person. This upfront investment of time should pay rich dividends and provide the opportunity to help people" (*The Expanded Mission of City Center Churches*, International Urban Associates, © 1998, pp. 53-54) Making inroads into a community really depends on who you know. Networking is the means of meeting and relating with people who don't know you and your ministry. Effective networkers are initiators. They take the responsibility on their own shoulders to make themselves known.

When I was planting my church, I would intentionally pop in on the mayor and other civic leaders. Many times they weren't in or available and I would leave my business card and a message with their assistants. This small act communicated many things: that I valued them as individuals, respected their positions, and desired to serve and care for the larger community. Many times I have received comments from people in our church who met these community leaders, and they have had nothing but positive things to say about me and my ministry. This is a principle we call the "Getting power people to say positive things about you." David J. Hesselgrave stresses the importance of this activity:

> Research in the areas of anthropology, sociology and communication underscores the importance of the roles of formal leaders, sponsors and mediators in society. Depending upon the particular societal arrangements that appertain, the newcomer may find it all but impossible to gain acceptance apart from proper approach to such persons. Even in Western societies that emphasize egalitarianism, an initial contact with those who fill these roles will usually enhance the missionary cause.
>
> (*Planting Churches Cross-Culturally: A Guide for Home and Foreign Missions*, Baker Publishing Group, © 1980, p. 167)

Effective networkers know how to make a positive first impression. They understand their environment and know want is acceptable and unacceptable conversation and attire. They know how to get people to talk about themselves, their business, their desires and dreams. They know how to tell who they are and what they do in twenty-five words or less, in a way that draws questions out of others. There is nothing more annoying than people who just talk about themselves and show very little interest in others. Networkers are effective listeners and are continually learning about the nuances of their communities and the leaders who serve them.

Networkers take every referral seriously. They know how to follow up on people quickly. Once I was given a name by a fellow church planter from another community. I followed up on it within 48 hours and saw the husband return to Christ and the wife come to Christ. And I got my first keyboard player, too! In another instance I followed up promptly on a lead of a business leader who needed to sell some property because of a financial hardship. This eventually led to the church purchasing 55 acres of prime property.

Networkers are willing to try something new. They put themselves in new situations and new circles of people. Many of my church planters join the local Chamber of Commerce and take the next step by volunteering to join a sub committee. Darryn Scheske of Heartland Church, Fishers, Indiana, joined the Business and Government Relations Committee. Within a year he knew all of the top political and business leaders in his community, and he was asked to open the Indiana State House of Representatives in prayer for their opening session. Not bad for a guy who didn't know a soul one year prior.

3. Be available to those experiencing life transitions.

George Hunter III, in his book *Spreading the Power* (Abingdon, © 1987), states "Persons experiencing important life transitions are more receptive than persons in stable periods of life. In every season, many people are experiencing some major change in their lives or social roles, and this tends to 'unfreeze' their lives and makes change possible." He then lists the kinds of transitions that increase a persons receptivity: "adolescence, going to college (or the armed forces), first job, getting married, first child, last child leaving home, menopause, mid-life crisis, retirement, loss of loved one, and other similar experiences. Additional receptivity-inducing transitions that many people experience include birth (or adoption) of a sibling, moving to a new community, getting fired, job advancement, separation, divorce and second marriage." Hunter continues, "Notice that not all these transition are necessarily experienced as 'crises.' Nontraumatic transitions can still induce receptivity" (p. 84).

Over my years of ministry I have seen many people embrace Christ as Lord and Savior just because I was available: The young God-fearing couple who desired to get married in a church that was acceptable to their parents and discovered the liberating joy of knowing Jesus. The single mom whose hospital stay in a new community opened her heart to the comfort of Christ. The woman who suffered multiple miscarriages and experienced the healing mercy of Jesus and became an effective servant of Christ, now blessed with two beautiful children. The couple whose teenager was out of control and discovered that they had a void in their souls that only Jesus could satisfy.

As leaders we understand that there are times when we just have to push ourselves out there to be available. We experience weariness of being on call and the labor of tilling the soil in hospital calls, premarital counseling, counseling sessions, and crisis interventions. Yet when we look back, we don't remember the weariness, but rather the names of those who met Jesus in a transition point and are still walking with him today. The Apostle John wrote, "I have no greater joy than to hear that my children are walking in the truth" (3 John 4). To experience that joy, to experience being a part of God's work, and to experience the glory of Christ entering a soul still drives us to be available.

4. Share your wins, losses, and blunders continually with the church.

A great definition of evangelism that I find myself gravitating toward is from Bill Fay. He says, "Success isn't leading someone to Christ. Success is acting out your Christian life, sharing the gospel, and trusting God for the results." Church planters Bob and Cynthia Schuler of Hartford, Wisconsin, have a family tradition. At the beginning of each new year they write a list of the people they want to come to faith in Christ during the next twelve months. They seal the list in an envelope and they pray for God's mercy on the lives whose names are recorded. Then, on December 31 they open the envelope to see what God has done. Often, says Bob, those people have come to know the Savior. Those types of stories encourage us to push back against evangelism entropy. As leaders, let's continue to share our stories of success with those around us. They are vital in reminding us of our vision and ultimate purpose.

But let's not just share our victories. Let's share our blunders, too. Too many times we set our people up with unrealistic expectations by sharing only the evangelistic wins and not all the hard work, waiting, and lengthy discussions that go into seeing one soul brought into the kingdom of light. We need to tell of the times when we pressed too hard for a decision and lost relational credibility. And we should admit the episodes when we had the opportunity to share a verbal witness and yet held back for some reason. One highly successful church planter told a revealing story:

> Many of us want to learn how to say just the right words that will persuade and convince our friends and family members that there is nothing better than walking with Jesus. But the truth is that one of the main reasons that people reject Christianity is not because they reject the message — it's because so many people who carry the name of Jesus are such poor representatives of him. And as a result, people decide that the message of Christianity lacks truth and power because it seems to make so little difference in the lives of its adherents.

> As we deal with the topic of sharing our faith with others, most people would assume that for a pastor, sharing my faith must be very easy for me and that I'm probably wildly successful in leading hundreds and hundreds of people into a relationship with Jesus Christ.

> The truth is, it is a real struggle for me. That's not to say that I don't consider it a great privilege to share the truth and hope of Jesus with others, and it's not to say that I haven't had the unmatched joy of being used of God to guide someone into a relationship with the

Savior. However, it is still very hard for me, and if I'm honest, I would have to say that I fail far more often than I succeed.

Two weeks after Michelle and I were first married, we moved to Pittsburgh where we knew no one, and I had my first job as a director of student ministries in a large church. Those first few years for Michelle and me as a married couple were really difficult, and we struggled through a lot of frustration and disillusionment in our first couple of years and even had a few "animated conversations."

I share this with you because on the floor above our apartment building was a young couple named John and Laurie. We had become friends with them, shared our faith in Christ with them, and even had them out to church with us. Their level of spiritual interest seemed to really be growing, and then suddenly, it seemed to shut off. We were confused.

Some time later, I went door-to-door in our apartment building inviting people out to a special event we were having at our church. While I was upstairs, I knocked on the apartment door which was next door to our friends John and Laurie. An older woman came to the door that I had never met. I introduced myself, told her that I lived on the floor below, and invited her to the church event. She said, "You live on the floor below?"

I said "Yes."

She said, "Then you must be the one I've heard raising his voice with his wife. Are you guys doing O.K.?"

I was horrified. That was thirteen years ago, and it was the first wake-up call that told me I had anger problems, and needed to learn how to handle them. I was ashamed as I realized that I had been treating my wife so poorly, and I was embarrassed that someone else was aware of it. After she closed the door, I glanced to the right and saw John and Laurie's door. Suddenly a thought occurred to me. Maybe the fire of their interest in spiritual things was put out by my behavior. Maybe they decided there was no truth and no power in the Christian message because of my bad example.

I was crushed inside. And if He wanted to, God could have and should have recalled me, as a representative of His, right at that moment.

Evangelism entropy is a reality in the Christian life, even among church planters. Like bodily exercise, it isn't as natural to us as it maybe should be. So we need to push back against the entropy, to train ourselves to do what is right. We need to find ways to be reinvigorated for the cause. Otherwise, we're found standing alone in a minefield.

Questions to Ponder (While Standing in This Minefield)

In which areas do I struggle with burnout or balance?

How am I cultivating my mission field with prayer?

How would I evaluate my networking skills?

What actions can I take to upgrade my networking?

What action steps can I take to be in the path of receptive people?

How have I communicated my evangelistic wins and losses with others?

LANDMINE 5:
CORPORATE EVANGELISM ENTROPY

Unless the church evangelizes, it fossilizes!
A. G. Gorden

*I care not where I go, or how I live, or what I endure so that I may save souls.
When I sleep, I dream of them; when I awake, they are first in my thoughts*
David Brainerd

"What is the one thing that if it doesn't happen in the first year of this new church will greatly disappoint you?" That was the question Mark Albrecht, of Northbridge Church of Antioch, Illinois, asked as he sat down with his launch team a week before their grand opening service. Everyone replied in kind: "If we don't see anyone come into a saving relationship with Jesus Christ, we'll be terribly disappointed."

There is nothing better than to have a highly motivated team of leaders focused on reaching those far from Christ. And yet statistics and our experience reveal that evangelism entropy can creep deep inside a new church within months of its first public service. The longer we are around new churches, the more amazed we are at how quickly these mission-focused, vibrant new churches become old. A. G. Gorden had it right many years ago when he said, "Unless the church evangelizes, it fossilizes!"

Understanding Reasons for Corporate Entropy

If church planting leaders are going to navigate this landmine, they must understand some of the reasons why the church drifts into a nonevangelistic mode. First, there is postpartum syndrome. After the intensity of the birth there is always some type of let down. I remember gathering and working with my launch team for nine months, articulating and modeling the value of evangel-ism. Within a month of seeing the church triple in size, one of those same launch team members came to me and said, "I don't care about all these new people, all I care about is the core group!" I was perplexed at how a person who prayed, planned, worked, and dreamed of this could say such a thing, only four months later. It seems that the enemy uses this postpartum syndrome to shift the focus of the church (in a heartbeat!) from mission to maintenance.

A second reason for a new church drifting into maintenance is that it may have had an ineffective launch, or grand opening. We've come up with at least twelve reasons why this may happen: 1. Sometimes church planters don't think a grand opening is necessary. They have a bias against creating momentum. I simply ask those church planters to read Acts 1-2. And then I ask, "How did God launch the church?" He had a specific group of spiritually empowered leaders who, at a specific time, were used to create interest in the things of God. The event generated spiritual questions, God-centered answers, the hope of forgiveness, and an explosion of conversion growth. 2. Another possible expla-nation for a poor launch is that the church was birthed prematurely. The launch team was not developed enough in terms of critical mass and critical roles. 3. Sometimes the spiritual warfare of starting a new church is underestimated. Prayer, fasting, and the spiritual disciplines were not taken seriously. 4. There was no evangelism during the prenatal phase. The evangelistic DNA was never set properly. 5. Launch team members did not participate in an adequate inviting strategy. Many potential contacts were ignored. 6. Marketing efforts were targeted to the wrong group. (It amazes me how many new churches advertise on Christian radio and Christian newspapers!) 7. There was no contacting strategy of newcomers and new movers in the community. The new church plant ignores this vitally receptive group. 8. Marketing is overly depend-ent on canned marketing pieces. People know a canned piece when they see it. In fact, they've probably seen it before. 9. There simply was not enough marketing exposure. We recommend a minimum of 20,000 direct marketing pieces (in communities with that many households) or at least two weeks of radio ads on secular radio. Or, both! 10. The date of the launch was poorly planned. Many church planters launched on the Sunday of the switch to daylight savings time or on a Sunday that conflicts with a major local event. (We have discovered that the two best times to launch in North America are early fall or one month prior to Easter.) 11. The worship experience was not meaningful for the target group. Darryn Scheske of Heartland Church, Fishers, Indiana, raised enough money to pay for professional musicians until enough volunteers were developed. Many church planters recruit other churches to provide child-care and children's programs until they develop their own volunteers. 12. Poor preaching is related to this. It is amazing how many church planters get consumed with all the details of launch and then remember at the last minute that they have to preach that Sunday. We encourage our church planters to have six to twelve months of series and message titles prepared and to have the first series ready to go. And practice, practice, practice!

A properly executed grand opening can yield three to four times the size of the launch team. If you have 40 adults on your launch team, you can usually attract between 160 and 200 attendees, with 50 percent of those being unchurched seekers.

The third reason for corporate evangelistic entropy is what is known as the "tyranny of the urgent." Stephen Covey, in his classic book *Seven Habits of Highly Effective People* (Free Press, © 1990) says there are two factors that determine activity: urgency and importance. Urgent items are those that are

> requiring immediate attention. It's 'Now!' Urgent things act on us. ...
> Urgent matters are usually visible. They press on us. They insist on action. They're often popular with others. They are usually right in front of us. And often they are pleasant, easy, and fun to do. But so often unimportant! (pp. 150-51)

Covey describes important as "...being focused on results. If something is important, it contributes to your mission, your values, and your high priority goals. Important matters that are not urgent require more initiative, more proactivity." Let's consider the urgent/important matrix as it relates to the first six months of a new church:

	Urgent	Non-Urgent
Important within the First Six Months	**Activities** Pastoral Care needs Logistical problems Launch team fallout Leadership backlash	**Activities** Sermon preparation Strategic evangelism Events Follow up process Assimilation plan working Leadership development process
Not important within the First Six Months	**Activities** Interruptions Popular activities Meetings Expanding ministries	**Activities** Establishment of missions committee Launching new ministries

One key to seeing your way through this landmine is a well thought-out timeline that both reflects your strategic plan and key events. We have our church planters submit a church planting proposal before we hire them. It amazes us how many times we have to ask them to bring it out and dust it off.

This should be on their desk — and in their people's hands — to help keep the entire project focused on the important, while making room to handle the urgent wisely.

Equipping: A Strategy for Overcoming Corporate Entropy

Continual equipping of your people will make a big difference in overcoming corporate evangelism entropy. Such equipping will help them reach the people in their networks through praying, sharing, inviting, bringing, and including. Following are several components of effective equipping:

1. Fueling the prayer life of your people

George Barna writes, "A church that strives to evangelize its community without saturating its efforts in prayer is like a race-car driver that jumps into his car at the starting line and discovers that the tank has not been filled with gasoline" (*Evangelism That Works*, Regal Books, © 1995, p. 128) How does a church planter keep the evangelism tank filled with prayer? One way is for them to create a weekly email prayer letter to the new church family. It doesn't need to be long and fancy, but it should be motivational enough to encourage the development of an outward-focused prayer life. Over the years I have collected hundreds of prayer quotes, and I always include one at the beginning of my e-prayer letter. This helps to create a culture of God-dependence.

One excellent discipline is to have your people create and submit prayer lists of those they want to see come to Christ. We train our church planters to do this. They ask their people to bring these lists to launch team meetings so that every name can be verbally lifted up to God in prayer. We start with five names from each person with a goal of helping them to identify 25 individuals who would be targeted to invite to the first public worship service. If a church planter has 40 adults on their launch team, a potential pool of 1000 people has been prayed for! This practice seems to die off after the launch, but it could easily be revived in small group or leadership team settings.

Related to prayer is the discipline of fasting. Joel 1:14 commands, "Declare a holy fast; call a sacred assembly. Summon the elders and all who live in the land to the house of the Lord your God, and cry out to the Lord." Calling the church to fast is the responsibility of spiritual leaders. There are variants of the fasting discipline, some of which are discussed in chapter 8. It's erroneous to think that new churches cannot be challenged to fast. Even leaders of seeker-driven church models need to know that we call them "seekers" for a reason. They are seeking, whether they know it or not, the things of God. In this case, the church is seeking God to reveal himself to those who need him most.

Finally, consider the creation of prayer cells that meet throughout the week. When Tom was a pastor, he had an early morning prayer meeting each

Wednesday that focused exclusively on outreach. It yielded impressive results, as intercessors truly learned to lean on God.

2. Training your people to be storytellers

In his book *Evangelism Outside the Box* (IVP, © 2000), Rich Richardson emphasizes the importance of storytelling in our postmodern era. "Storytelling helps follow the rules of experiential truth." In other words, telling stories makes sense both emotionally and experientially to our audience. He continues, "If something rings true for us experientially and we can be authentic and non-manipulative in the way we tell the story, people will respond" (p. 93). There is nothing more powerful than the fresh story of a new convert. This is the first story your people should learn to share—and they should learn to share it well. And don't make the mistake of waiting too long before teaching your converts to tell their story. Some sort of evangelism training should be offered on a routine basis (perhaps monthly), so that every believer learns the basics of sharing their story — and sharing THE story.

Evangelism training should include teaching believers how to tell their faith story. A simple three-part guideline like this can serve as a template to help them write their testimony:

Before I made a faith commitment to Jesus, I experienced …

I realized I needed to trust and follow Jesus when …

Since entrusting my life to Christ, I have experienced …

Darryn Scheske of Heartland Church in Fishers, Indiana, offers some great wisdom that he shares while training his people to share their faith stories:

Never give away the answer to salvation in your personal testimony too early.

Do not go into detail about former sins.

Be specific (as compared to vague, i.e. "I was lost, but now I'm found").

Be humble (God is to be exalted, not you).

Be brief (this isn't a sermon!)

Don't be overly dramatic (This isn't Acting 101).

Get rid of the "Christian-ese" (i.e. "I've been washed in the blood").

Never argue or put down anyone or any religion.

Be careful not to inadvertently criticize the life of the person you are sharing with.

End your testimony with your favorite Scripture and a brief comment on why that text has been meaningful to you.

We encourage church planters to require a written testimony for church membership, for baptism candidates, and for all those desiring to participate in a child dedication ceremony. In the materials that I've developed (see *www.yourjourney.org*), new Christians will have written their story at least three times by the time they finish their first ten lessons. Don't ignore the power of a well-told faith story!

Storytelling doesn't stop with the individual's conversion report. A second story that your people must be prepared to tell is the story of your church. The miraculous story of the birth of a new church can generate a plethora of spiritual discussions. For fundraising purposes, church planters should be able to tell their vision in less than a minute. We encourage the same standard for your church members: in less than a minute they should be able to articulate the reasons why the church got started, its unique vision, and how and why they became involved.

Both Tom and I work in raising up new church planters. When people ask us what we do for a living, our response always leads to a spiritual discussion. There is something intriguing about new things, including new churches. Pastors, don't miss this! Equip your people to tell the story of your church and its impact on their lives!

The third story you want to your people to know well is the Master's story. To do this, they first must learn how to get into spiritual discussions and to find spiritually receptive people. Too much of our evangelism training is geared toward those who are hostile and unreceptive to the gospel. When Jesus sent seventy-two disciples to share his story, his instruction was, "When you enter a house, first say 'Peace to this house.' If a man of peace is there, your peace will rest on him: if not, it will return you" (Luke 10:5-6). There was something in the statement "Peace to this house" that alerted the evangelists to spiritual receptivity. A quick look at the receptivity barometer determined whether the discussion would continue or the evangelist would move on.

How can we determine the receptivity barometer today? One method that I stumbled into was to ask, "Do you believe people are on a spiritual journey?" If they responded positively, I'd begin to describe what that journey would look like in relation to Jesus. Over time, I developed a visual aid where, in my presence, people would be asked to point to where they were on their journey. There are a number of options: Not Interested, Curiously Interested, Assertively Searching, or At the Cross. On the other side of the cross there are more options: Actively Following, Growing in Fellowship, Making an Impact. See page 88 for a sample of the Journey Guide.

I then bring the seeker through four diagnostic questions:

1. Where are you now on your spiritual journey?

2. Where would you like to be on your spiritual journey in six months to a year?

3. What barriers are between you and that point?

4. What will it take for you to remove those barriers?

This is a form of spiritual diagnosis, where we can discover how deeply the Holy Spirit is at work in a person's life. The goal is not to lead people toward a prayer of repentance but to help them recognize their barriers and develop a personalized plan for spiritual discovery or spiritual maturity.

I hope you see how important this step of diagnosis is. We want our people to enter into spiritual discussions with receptive people. Upon diagnosis we can then proceed with a clear presentation of the gospel. There are many fine tools: The Romans' Road, The Four Spiritual Laws, The Bridge, Steps to Peace with God, and one I developed called "How Can I Get Close to God?" Choose a tool that works for you and make it the standard for your church. Then train, train, train.

Pastor John Jenkins of First Baptist Church in Glenarden, Maryland, says that one of the reasons their mega-church has seen so much conversion growth over the last fifteen years is that every one of his staff, deacons, employees, and members of his church have been thoroughly trained to lead someone to Christ or back to Christ through the use of the Romans' Road. He once said to me, "Our people should learn to do the Roman's Road in their sleep!" Don't overwhelm your people with too many methods. Determine a standard for your church and drive it home. Soon your people will be able to communicate it with authenticity and ease.

3. Training your people to be inviters and includers

Statistics show that one out of four adults in the United States will go to church if someone invites them (George Barna, *Marketing the Church*, NavPress, © 1988, p. 111). Equipping your people to be inviters and includers will be critical to getting past the corporate evangelism entropy landmine.

Rich Richardson speaks of the need for "soul-awakening events" in the life of the church. Such events

> …awaken people to the existence of their soul. These events get people in touch with their spiritual needs and longings. These events do not call people to conversion. A quick call to conversion is not good stewardship to people who are still a long way from God. It turns them off. It pushes them away…. I am convinced that high-quality soul-awakening events are the greatest missing link in evangelism today. I am also convinced that high-quality soul-awakening events will be the most controversial part of what vibrant evangelistic ministries do. (*Evangelism Outside the Box*, IVP, © 2000, p. 76)

If we are to form an army of inviters, let's consider some categories of soul-awakening events that are invite-worthy.

Worship Services and Special Events

Worship services are the first area of focus. Some seeker-driven churches say that every Sunday is an opportunity to invite your seeker friends and family. Other churches pick one Sunday a month and declare it to be especially seeker-focused. Others adapt the Big Sunday approach where three to five times each year they encourage their people to pray and invite their friends and family. This approach might focus on children's Christmas productions, Christmas Eve, Easter Sunday, Mother's Day, some type of summer event, and a fall kickoff event.

The church I planted hosted a Friendship Sunday every summer, inviting a Christian sports figure or local television personality to give a credible testimony. Along with this, we put on a huge family fun picnic, with a petting zoo, pony rides, and — my personal favorite — rides on Lulu the elephant! The entire aim of this event was to celebrate our friendships and explore what a friendship with Jesus would look like. Other churches do three or four strategic sermon series each year that speak to the soul of our culture by introducing biblical truth to subjects as healthy relationships, intimacy, meaning-of-life issues, family, marriage, and work. Doing soul-awakening events in the context of your worship services brings a huge advantage. They provide easy access to the community, they typically draw a crowd (which brings a sense of credibility), and they carry a low "threat threshold," making it easy to invite others.

A foundational element to these soul awakening events is to provide something that will ignite the inviters in your church. Ask yourself the question "Would I risk inviting my neighbors, my unchurched friends, and my family to these events?" Another element is to provide opportunities for your people to include unchurched friends in the actual production of these events. Encourage your musicians to invite their musician friends. Have your actors include fellow actors. Your tech people should ask for the expertise of their techy friends. One year the bass section of our choir was filled with seekers who committed to attending rehearsals and performed at our Christmas musical. Recently at the launch of one of our new churches a professional sound technician was invited and ended up rescuing this infant church with thousands of dollars of his company's own equipment. He hasn't missed a Sunday since.

Fishing Pool or Affinity Group Events

"Fishing pool" events are typically built around affinity groups. Men's, women's, and single's ministries can sponsor wonderful events that specifically target the needs of their group. Right now I'm in charge of our new church's monthly Saturday morning men's breakfast. In the past, we have seen churches put on golf outings for golfers, wild game dinners for hunters, fishing retreats for fishermen, and leadership seminars for business leaders. Many men have come into a relationship with Christ through these fishing pool events. I remember one man who came to a wild game dinner. It was his first contact with our church, and over the course of that year he made his way into the life of the church and embraced Christ as Savior. One year later he shared his testimony at the wild game dinner. His opening line was "My spiritual journey started one year ago at this same event."

Let your imagination be your guide:

Marriage seminars and retreats for couples.

Cooking and decorating seminars for the chefs and decorators in your area.

Children's productions for the unchurched children in your neighborhood.

Adventure trips (rock climbing, canoeing, etc.) for those risk-takers in your network.

Sporting events for the athletes in your community.

In my men's ministry we are planning a father/son event with a five-time Super Bowl participant who will share his faith story. There is no shortage of great ideas!

Following are some basics to consider in making these fishing pool events effective: 1. They need to be fun. They need to a have an atmosphere that is filled with laughter, enthusiasm, and positive energy. Laughter and fun reduce tension and build a relaxing atmosphere that allows people to open themselves up to others and to God's influence on their lives. Attendees should take away good and positive memories, which will only build momentum for the future. 2. They need to be meaningful on two levels. First, on a pragmatic level, the event needs to deliver what it promises. If you advertise a marriage seminar, there had better be some good help for marriages. Second, on a spiritual level, don't shy away from having someone share a meaningful faith story or have a teaching moment where a biblical truth is conveyed in a practical way. Since the event is sponsored by a church, there is a level of expectancy that something spiritual will be included. Just make it good, attractive, and not over-bearing. 3. They need to provide meaningful connections with others. In putting on many men's events over the years, I am continually amazed that the number one thing men appreciate is time to sit around a table with some other men like themselves and talk about life, family, and faith. You will need to build into your events some type of connecting moment where people can open up and reflect on what they have just experienced. Simple, nonthreatening discussion questions can open up some amazing doors. I recommend getting a hold of a Serendipity Bible as a resource for dozens and dozens of discussion questions.

Small Groups

My journey in the area of small groups has taken me down many paths and led me to wonderful encounters. As a pioneer church planter, I was always looking for opportunities to share the gospel and build relationships. I remember interacting with a young seeker couple who was interested in the faith but had not yet trusted Christ. The Bible was basically a foreign book to them. So we set up the next four Tuesday nights for the purpose of introducing them to the Bible. From that opportunity, over the next five years through many hits and misses, I developed a basic curriculum called Bible 101. The purpose was to introduce individuals to the Bible by weaving in the story of the Savior throughout the study. During this time I discovered that many people were afraid of small Bible study groups because they knew nothing about the Bible and were embarrassed by that fact. By calling these seeker Bible studies Bible 101, we attracted classes of serious seekers every time we started them.

Another thing I discovered through this process was that in the third of the four weeks many of these serious seekers asked the question "Do we need to quit after next week's study?" There is something very powerful in gathering serious seekers together and seeing the Holy Spirit warm their hearts. So instead of ending the study at week four, I developed another four-week study called "Christianity 101," which was designed to introduce them to the person and work of Jesus Christ. When that study was completed, we would simply go through the Gospel of John using the inductive study method we had learned in Bible 101. Within six months to a year, I saw many of these seeking communities turned into believing communities.

Here are a few insights to help build effective seeker studies: 1. Never start a group without having an apprentice leader alongside the leader. Always have a teachable pre-leader in the wings. 2. Keep it simple. Do not overwhelm the group with study guides and cumbersome curricula. The biblical content does not need to be deep to be profound. Stick to the basics. When introducing people to the Old Testament, for example, I have them read Isaiah 53 as a group. Then I ask the question, "Whom do you think the prophet is speaking about?" They'll all correctly say, "Jesus." Then I communicate to them that this was written 700 years before his birth, and that they can go to Israel and see a copy of Isaiah's scroll that is dated at least 250 years before Christ's birth. (There are times that someone in the group wants further information to investigate an issue deeper. This is where a good resource list comes in handy to help that person take the next step. But in most case I would encourage you to keep it simple.) 3. Never host the group at your home or the home of your apprentice. The most effective groups are started in seekers' homes. I remember asking an unmarried couple who I knew were living together at the time to host a Bible 101 class in their home. Some people in our church found out about it and were appalled that we would hold a Bible study in the home of people who were "living in sin." I replied to criticism by saying, "I think you have it wrong. I believe that only believers can willfully live in sin. They have at one time acknowledged and accepted the truth, but they're now rebelling and rejecting it. I believe these seekers are under the wrath of God and we need to go to them where they are and present God's truth to them." Within a year the couple that hosted that study trusted Christ as Savior and began following him as Lord. I had the privilege of baptizing them and performing their wedding.

Equipping your people is vital to overcoming evangelistic entropy. Equipping is like keeping your foot on the gas pedal of your car. Once you take your foot off the pedal, you'll start to slow down. Consequently, you'll need to rev your engine to expend more effort to get back to your original speed. A number of years ago I heard Bill Hybels speak from his heart on this issue. He said that during the first fifteen years of Willow Creek's ministry they saw large numbers of conversion growth. Then they took their foot off the evangelistic gas pedal for a number of reasons. He continued with tears in his eyes, saying how hard it was to get up to speed again. I have never forgotten that moment! Church planters: let's keep the evangelistic pedal to the metal for the glory of God!

Questions to Ponder (While Standing in This Minefield)

What might cause our new church to lose its evangelism edge?

What are the critical non-urgent/important issues for us right now?

What will we intentionally neglect?

Which evangelistic tool will we adopt as our bread-and-butter?

What new fishing pool ideas can we try?

LANDMINE 6:

INADEQUATE ENFOLDING STRATEGY

God creates men, but they choose each other.
Niccolo Machiavelli

Hey, what do I do now?" We have heard these words come out of the mouths of many church planters within weeks of launching their new church. It usually happens in week three, when they realize that every week new people are walking into their worship services and many are walking out the back door. Launching a new church is so event-oriented, with the planning and preparation of the public worship services, that something is likely to suffer. In this case it's the landmine of poor follow-up of newcomers.

The damage this landmine can do to a new church often depends on how well its worship services are received. If they are not as effective in drawing a critical mass, from 75 to 100 people, the damage can be life-threatening. It's axiomatic that the smaller the launch, the more critical it is for a well-defined and well-executed follow-up plan. If a church launch is effective (over 200 people), poor follow-up can be hidden by the success of the launch and the excitement of the crowd. However, even in those cases if the issue of follow-up and enfolding is not addressed, a price will be paid before too long. To stick with our landmine metaphor, it can be like an undetected piece of shrapnel that leads to infection, internal bleeding, and a lingering death.

In order to appropriately address the landmine of follow-up, planters must first have a clear picture of where their church is headed. In the movie *Forrest Gump*, starring Tom Hanks, Forrest said, "If you don't know where you are going, you won't know where you are when you get there." In our opinion, many church planters have a romantic vision of church planting, and they struggle with the issue of how to turn their new church over to their converts. Following up, nurturing, and empowering new converts is a messy business. This is why a clear strategy is needed before the new church opens its doors, and the strategy needs to be revisited and reworked again and again.

Let's begin by looking at two macro principles: (1) discipleship, or spiritual formation and (2) ministry flow. Following that, we'll look at six micro principles that you can immediately apply to your situation.

Discipleship

Jesus said to his disciples, "Therefore go and make disciples of all nations, baptizing them in the name of the Father and of the Son and of the Holy Spirit, and teaching them to obey everything I have commanded you. And surely I am with you always, to the very end of the age" (Matthew 28:19-20, NIV). There is a lot of confusion around the issue of disciple making. If church planters can work through this issue early, they will be well on their way toward their ultimate objective of seeing lives changed.

Nothing grates our nerves more than when we hear churches, pastors or lay people say "We are great at discipleship and terrible at evangelism." I heard this story from a church planter who was experiencing great conversion growth. He was asked by a large church to come and consult them on becoming more evangelistically effective. They said, "We need your help because we are great at discipleship but very weak at evangelism." He responded, "If you are great at discipleship, why do you need me?" They answered, "Because we are ineffective in reaching lost people, yet strong in discipling believers." Again the church planter responded, "I still don't understand. If you are great at discipling believers why do you need me?" This frustrating exchange continued a few more times until the church leader realized he and his church had an inadequate view of discipleship — and that, in reality, they were terribly weak at discipleship.

Many churches, leaders, and church planters eventually drift into this mentality because they equate discipleship with the tidy teaching of facts and dispensing of information. Such a pattern only reproduces the tidy teaching and dispensing of information, instead of, as George Barna puts it, reproducing "zealots for Christ" (*Growing True Disciples*, Waterford Press, © 2001, p. 20).

Let's consider one helpful definition of evangelism that can lay the foundation for an effective outreach and enfolding strategy: "Evangelism is communicating the gospel in an understandable manner and motivating a person to respond to Christ and become a responsible member of his church" (*A Practical Encyclopedia of Evangelism and Church Growth*, Regal, © 1996, p. 205).

I believe this is a good start, but it needs to be expanded. I suggest the following: Disciple making is communicating the gospel with clarity and conviction, so that people can embrace Christ as Lord and Savior and become reproducing followers serving within a healthy community of faith.

The following diagram helps delineate disciple making as both a decision and a process. Based on the words of Jesus from Matthew 28:19, the diagram illustrates the multifaceted reality of "making disciples of all nations."

Relating – "go … nations." The text is better translated "as you go" or "as you are going", meaning "wherever your travels take you in this life" — even to the ends of the earth. This reveals the need to build genuine rapport and to authentically relate with your neighbors, your community, and your world. In other words, we place ourselves in the flow of what God is doing.

Reaching/conversion – "make disciples." A friend of mine once told me that if you truly embrace Christ as Lord and Savior you will see God's work happening right before your eyes. I like the way Brian McLaren states it: "Count conversations, not just conversions" (*More Ready Than You Realize*, p. 135). Do we really believe that "the Father is drawing people to himself?" Our work is in the conversations, God's work is in the converting.

Identifying – "baptizing." Elmer Towns writes, "Effective evangelism implies winning people in a community and into a community, not just winning them as isolated individuals" (ASCG Journal 13: p. 45). Effectively calling people to publicly identify with Christ and to a community of Christ followers is essential to fulfilling the Great Commission. This is a foundational piece of anyone's spiritual formation

Training – "teaching them to obey." Dispensing information is easy. Training people is difficult. Imparting data is simple. Training people is messy. Jesus spent three years training his followers with a combination of sermons, private talks, special assignments, general tasks, observation, feedback, encouraging pep-talks, question asking, and modeling. Jesus spent three years experiencing the joy, pain, and utter frustration of training and shaping the values of his disciples.

Reproducing – "all I have commanded you." "All I have commanded you" includes this very command. Our obedience will naturally lead us to seeing others embrace the passion and the skills necessary to become effective disciple makers. We see this in the disciples themselves. Compare the Great Commission in Matthew 28:19-20 to the disciples' initial fulfillment, in Acts 2:36-47. The end product was a reproducing community of faith that ultimately experienced the Lord "adding to the numbers daily" (Acts 2:47).

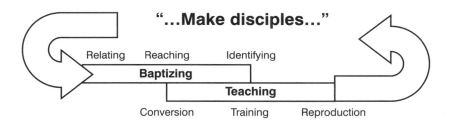

"…Make disciples…"

Relating   Reaching   Identifying

Baptizing

Teaching

Conversion   Training   Reproduction

Brian McLaren wrestles with this issue:

> I believe evangelism may be a less and less useful term in the future. I find myself replacing it more and more with the term disciple-making. I have noticed a progression going on. In a paradigm that is event-focused, we have evangelism and follow-up. Then we begin to feel that follow-up is a rather thin description of spiritual growth, and we speak of evangelism and discipleship, or evangelism and spiritual formation. But then when we see the dynamic, holistic and relational process overshadowing the single conversion event so that the event only has meaning for us within the larger process, we find ourselves speaking more and more in terms of disciple-making. And at that moment, something wonderful happens: We find ourselves transported out of stuffy class-rooms and air-conditioned church halls, our meetings and committees and liturgies and Bible studies. And we find ourselves touching down, blinking and wide-eyed, inside the wild world of gospel stories with Jesus and his original disci-ples … The world desperately needs a fresh emphasis on holistic discipleship process. (*More Ready Than You Realize*, Zondervan, © 2002, p. 161)

Ministry Flow

Once we move away from a dualistic approach of evangelism and disci-pleship to a holistic approach of disciple making, we can discuss the concept of ministry flow. This is the map work of disciple making. It is a transferable prin-ciple that needs to be understood and addressed in every church. Because we are dealing with church planters in a variety of settings, we strive to be more principle-centered in our training. We need to find principles that fit urban, rural, and suburban settings — principles that can transcend cultural and ideological settings. By dealing with Anglo, Vietnamese, Filipino, African-American, and Hispanic post-modern cultural groups — and in assisting those with a baby boomer mentality to those with an emerging church perspective — we are forced to look for the transferable ideas behind the successful models. The concept of ministry flow is one of those ideas.

Every new church reaches people through the front door (public worship services or soul-awakening events), side door (affinity events or small groups), and back door (one-on-one invitations or relational evangelism). The church that experiences exponential growth works all three doors very thoughtfully.

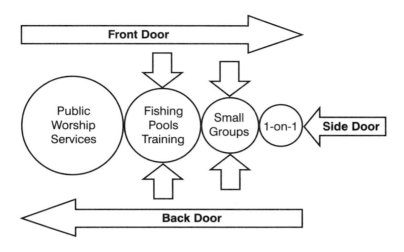

Grasping ministry flow will help develop focused ministries and programs that will leverage a new church's limited resources to obtain the greatest impact. In his book *Growing True Disciples*, George Barna writes, "Offering programs is not the issue. We discovered that surprisingly few churches have a well-conceived model of discipleship that they implement. The result is that churches feel they have fulfilled their obligation if they provide a broad menu of courses, events, and other experiences, but such a well-intentioned but disjointed approach leaves people confused and imbalanced." In our training events we challenge church planters to go beyond a gathering of people (public worship services) to design a unified plan for spiritual formation—one that matures converts into missionaries and spiritual leaders of the local church. We encourage them to develop a battle plan that will guide them as they engage in the mission of disciple making.

And as with any battle plan, there will need to be changes, adaptations, and retreats along the way. For instance, for close to twenty-five years Rick Warren's Saddleback Church has had a basic battle plan that has been reworked, changed, and retooled in order to effectively make disciples for Jesus. At one time Saddleback focused on only four purposes, but the plan was reworked to include the present-day five purposes of the church. We do well to remember that ministry flow is written in pencil, not in ink.

Micro Principles

Let's look at six specific things you can do immediately to improve your enfolding strategy.

1. First Impressions

Assimilation begins before a person walks into the church's meeting place. If a church is going to have a good disciple making process, it needs to take a serious look at the first impressions it makes on its potential disciples. Having good external and internal signage communicates that we care about newcomers. One planter we know has a long driveway that winds to the school the church meets in. Along the way they placed signs with simple messages like "Good Morning!" "We're Glad You're Here!", "God Loves You!" Having excellent greeter teams makes a great first impression, too. A smiling face in the parking lot, a warm welcome at the door, and a helpful assistant at the children's registration table all communicate that newcomers matter. When possible, escort newcomers with children to their rooms. Have a worship environment that is clean, pleasant, and welcoming. Your teams should be in place and on time. Make the worship program engaging, informative, and understandable. Good music helps determine the emotional atmosphere of the service. Having the right people on the platform often sets the tone and may determine if there will be a second chance to engage the visitor.

2. Response Filtering

Most churches have some type of registration process for newcomers. Guest books, registration pads, and information cards can gather basic data on visitors—in theory. In my experience these are being used ineffectively because church leaders do not understand the principle behind this idea: response filtering. Response filtering is a general term to describe the process of gathering data for specific follow-up of attendees. It recognizes that each person is on a spiritual journey, and the purpose of the church is to engage each person with regard to their journey (Dave Garrison, *Church Planting Movements*, p. 60.) Whatever method is used assumes that God is at work in their lives and that we, as a church, are responsible to minister to them appropriately.

But data-collecting mechanisms work only in theory. In church after church we hear the same questions, "How do we get people to respond?" or "How do you get people to fill out cards?" It's really not as hard as some think it is. Here are some suggestions.

a. Have a good descriptive title for the response card.

It is important to have a title for your response card. If you call it an Information Card, all you will get is information. If you call it a Visitor's Information Card, all you will get is visitor's information. Yet, if you call it a Communication Card or even, for example, NorthBridge Church Communication Card, you're positioned to do even more. This little card becomes one of the primary communication vehicles throughout the life of the church.

b. Design this communication card as an all-in-one tool for the entire church.

We believe every communication card should answer the following questions:

Who are they?

Include name, address, phone, email address, spouse's name and children's names with ages.

Have a box to check if they have already given you their contact information.

Which visit is it?

Offer these choices: First Time, Second Time, Third Time, or Regular Attender. (It is amazing how many people won't fill out the card until the third time attending the church.)

Do not have a space for "Member," which can create a sense of exclusiveness.

How did they hear about the church?

Offer such choices as Friend, Mail, Newspaper, Radio, Other. (This helps you measure the effectiveness of your marketing and inviting strategies.)

What are they interested in?

Offer such choices as Home Bible Studies, Recreational Activities, Children's Ministry, Youth Events, Help My Spiritual Journey. (Use simple, understandable terms; try to stay away from insider language.)

Do they want to sign up for specific classes, luncheons, or other events?

Have a list of letters on the card that are coded for specific events announced in your worship program. For example: "Party at the Pastor's House: September 26th at 6:00 pm. This is an opportunity for you to meet our pastoral staff in an informal setting. Space is limited, so if you would like to sign up, circle the letter "P" on your communication card.

What Sunday did they attend?

Have a place to insert the date. Or, if possible, have the date printed on the card already. This is important for follow-up, especially when delays occur.

Is there space to write questions, prayer requests, or their experience of the worship service?

Have plenty of space for them to respond in writing.

What, if any, spiritual decisions did they make? For example:

Today I put my trust in Jesus for the first time.

Today I recommitted myself to following Jesus.

What was their response to the message?

For example: Today's message has
inspired me to take action by _____.
raised a question regarding _____.
challenged my way of thinking by _____.
given me a new insight on _____.
helped me with _____.

c. Hand out pens.

If you want people to write things down give them something to write with. (This also comes in handy when they are going to write out a check for the offering!)

d. Have the card pointed out at least three times by three different people!

During mass evangelism services or soul-awakening events, we have learned that it takes at least three different people to point out the communication method at least once each during the service. Here is an example of a script that Mike Heiniger of Crossroads Community Church in Monticello, Illinois, wrote for his team.

Welcome (after the prelude)

Good morning. Welcome to Crossroads. My name is _____, and we're glad you're here today. In your message notes today we have a tear-off sheet we call our Connection Card. We like everyone to fill this out each week. This is one of the main ways we communicate with each other at Crossroads, and we take the time to read each one every week. If this is your first time with us, we would like to get to know you, and we would appreciate your comments as well.

Prayer Time (after the worship set)

We take praying for each other seriously here at Crossroads. If you have a personal prayer request, please let us know on the Connection Card today. Our prayer team will pray for each of these request this week. Join me as we pray this morning.

Offering (after the message)

As part of our service today, we worship God through the giving and receiving of our offerings. If this isn't your home church, or if this is your first time with us, we are not expecting you to give. You're our guest, and we appreciate you coming today. To let us know you were here, we'd appreciate receiving your Connection Card with any comments you have. As a way of saying thanks for coming today, we have a small gift for you. You can pick that up at our welcome table.

e. Train your people continually.

If you are going to create a culture of good communication in your church, you will need to train your people continually. Training involves instruction and positive reinforcement. Look for opportunities to instruct your people outside the service. One of my church planters uses his membership class as an opportunity to instruct his new members on the importance of the communication card. He passes them out during his class and asks everyone to fill them out. They all give him a strange look, but he insists. Once they finish, he explains why it is so important to the health of their church. Every healthy church thrives on good communication. He also explains why it is important for the completion of their mission as a church. If everyone (including members) fills out a card, then guests will feel comfortable, too.

Motivating people to use the communication card also involves positive reinforcement. Respond quickly to their questions, requests, and needs. Nothing cripples the process more than encouraging people to fill out a communication card without a sincere and timely response.

Another way to positively reinforce your communication method is to read the comments and answer the questions on the cards publicly. One church planter routinely takes such questions and addresses them in sermons or during a special question and answer time in the service.

Second Touch

Responding to those who come through our doors is a delicate matter that needs to be thought through seriously. We describe this as a second touch: all guests receive some type of contact from the church to acknowledge their presence and participation in the worship service. It can involve a response to a question, concern, or need. And it can be used to gather feedback from their visit. Responding to people can be measured in degrees with what we call the second touch thermometer.

90-100 – A gift delivered to their home by a volunteer before they get home after the service.

80-90 – A gift delivered to their home by a volunteer within 24 hours of their visit.

70-80 – A phone call from a volunteer within 48 hours of their visit.

60-70 – A gift delivered to their home by a volunteer within 48 hours of their visit.

50-60 – A phone call from the pastor or staff within 24 hours of their visit.

40-50 – A gift delivered to their home by the pastor or staff within 48 hours of their visit.

30-40 – A personalized letter from the pastor or staff addressing a specific question or concern, with appropriate materials enclosed. Example: What is child dedication?

20-30 – A personalized letter from the pastor or staff with a stamped First Impression Card enclosed.

10-20 – A personalized letter from the pastor or staff.

0 -10 – A form letter from the pastor or staff.

0 – No response

The issue here is that churches need to learn how to turn up the heat without turning off the visitor. One research project indicated that among high-assimilation churches the number of contacts or touches people received after their visit was four (Thom Rainer, High Expectations, Braodman, © 1999, p. 95). It is our conviction that churches that are afraid of overdoing it will always underachieve in this area. The study showed another interesting fact: 7 out of 10 visitors preferred a visit from a volunteer rather than from a member of the pastoral staff (p. 94). And the study revealed that there were rarely any complaints about unannounced visits from visitors (p. 95). My wife Mary leads the Second Touch Team at the new church we attend. She has delivered hundreds of gifts to newcomers and has heard only one complaint. On the other hand, she has dozens of compelling stories of how people received the gifts with joy and gratefulness. In many cases it made the difference in their taking the next step on their spiritual journey. Rainer concludes "If a person visits your church for the first time, the probability of their returning a second time is considerably higher if you make contact with them within thirty-six hours of their visit" (p. 96).

Second Touch Gift Ideas

- Homemade ccokies or bread
- Water bottles
- Custom coffee packets
- Coupons for discounts
- Microwave popcorn
- A book by the pastor

Next Steps

"Next steps" refers to understanding, communicating, and offering programming for the next step in someone's spiritual journey. It's easy to overlook this in the development of a new church. "Next steps" means taking the concept of ministry flow and making it understandable to the people—both seekers and believers—in your community. For example, when planning a "big Sunday" or a soul-awakening event, it's critical to include programming that helps all participants move to the next level on their spiritual journey. The following questions will help in navigating this issue:

What is your next step for seekers?

What is your next step for visiting believers?

What is your next step for regular attendees?

What is your next step for committed followers?

Lyle Schaller wrote, "From a long-term perspective the most influential single approach to increasing church attendance is to raise the level of expectations. All of us respond, in varying degrees, to the expectations others place on us" (Lyle E. Schaller, *44 Ways to Increase Church Attendance*, Abingdon, © 1988, p. 104). When we practice this principle, we are not only inviting people to take the next step but giving them specific markers that will guide them on their spiritual journey. Following is an example of how I practiced this principle in the church I planted. The idea is to offer a variety of options that can be customized to individuals, wherever they are.

1. The Next Steps for Seekers:

Bible 101 – A four-week introduction to the Bible, in a small group or classroom setting.

Christianity 101 – A 4-week introduction to the person and work of Jesus Christ, in a small group or classroom setting.

Newcomer's luncheon

Social events or affinity group meetings

Service opportunities

2. The Next Steps for Visiting Believers:

Newcomer's Luncheon –

Connection Class (membership)

Social events or affinity group meetings

Service opportunities

One-on-one mentoring

3. The Next Steps for Regular attendees:

Connecting with God's Family Class (membership)

Service opportunities

One-on-one mentoring

4. The Next Steps for Committed Members:

Cultivating Spiritual Maturity Seminar

Caring for Others through Spiritual Ministry Seminar

Communicating Christ to the World Seminar

Service opportunities

One-on-one mentoring

5. Modular Training

Modular training is a systematic approach to help new converts and believers work through spiritual formation issues, develop the necessary life/ministry skills, and make the critical commitments they need to move toward spiritual maturity and multiplication. This principle is built on the concept of learning by doing. David Hesselgrave provides the following insight:

> It is the fundamental law of pedagogy that one learns by doing. Learning is not simply a matter of cognition. It is also a matter of action. Learning that is divorced from life, that is only a matter of the accumulation of data, is hardly worthy of the name. The best education, therefore, is that which combines the classroom and the laboratory, that which involves the learner in the employment of information. Ted Ward sometimes uses the analogy of a split rail fence to communicate this approach to learning. The idea is that theory and practice go together and that periodically there should be an opportunity to discuss and analyze what one has learned and experienced. Though the "split rail diagram" with its reference to seminars and cognitive input seems especially applicable to colleges and universities, it would be a mistake to think that it does not apply to the local church and, indeed, to any learning situation. (David Hesselgrave, *Planting Churches Cross-Culturally*, Baker, © 1980, pp. 309-10)

Cognitive Input   Cognitive Input

Seminar   Seminar   Seminar

Experience   Experience

As the church grows, you will need to offer a variety of opportunities and settings to effectively reach and train those whom God has brought down your path. A large-group setting is anything with more than fifteen people. These can be seminars, classes, or even retreats. Small-group settings are for three to fifteen people.

One popular approach to modular training is Rick Warren's "purpose-driven church." This approach, described by a baseball diamond visual, allows for spiritual formation to occur in a variety of settings—for a variety of people.

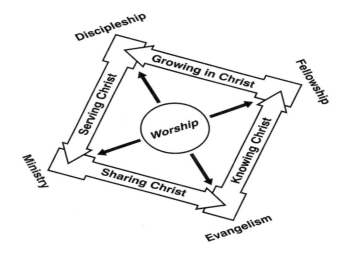

Touch Ministries is another example of the use of modular training combining mentoring, cell groups, and weekend retreats. Randall Neighbour uses the analogy of hiking up a mountain. He promotes the four-paths-and-four-camps methodology. Each path offers daily tools, a personal guide, and a community of believers to assist new believers in their spiritual formation. Each camp is a place where you find specific training and encouragement as you make your way up the mountain of discipleship and are launched into the world on a mission with Jesus. "The camps will be manned by staff members and mature volunteer leaders in your church. Any cell member who hikes up the discipleship trail will visit the camp, learn about the path ahead and pick up tools that will make the next part of the journey successful."

The camps are as follows, in order of use:

Spiritual Formation Weekend – Designed for new believers and members

Encounter God Retreat – Focused on deeper spiritual matters

Touching Hearts Weekend – Training in strategic and relational evangelism

Cell Leader Intern Retreat – Designed to mobilize and multiply cells group leaders.

(Source: *http://www.touchusa.org/how-to-disciple.asp*. Accessed November 2004)

I started a ministry called "Your Journey Resources." which is another example of the use of modular training in a one-on-one mentoring context. This process starts with a seeker or new believer and, through a series of daily assignments and mentoring sessions provides, a spiritual formation process with the goal of turning a curious seeker into a multiplying leader.

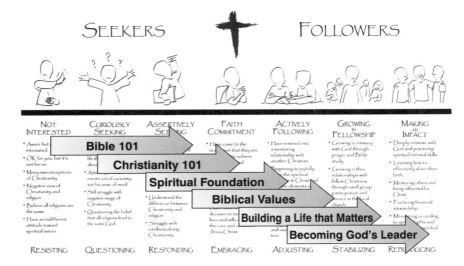

Step 1: Bible 101 – A four-week introduction to God's Word

Step 2: Christianity 101 – A four-week introduction to the person and work of Jesus Christ

Step 3: Developing a Spiritual Foundation — Ten lessons to engage new disciples in an in-depth training process to establish them in their new faith

Step 4: Discovering Biblical Values — Ten lessons that bring partici-pants through the basic doctrines of the Christian faith and help them turn these truths into personal values that guide their lives

Step 5: Building a Life that Matters — Ten lessons that help move a growing disciple from spiritual stability toward spiritual significance

Step 6: Becoming the Leader God Desires — Ten interactive lessons that help leaders see how the fruit of the Spirit flows through their leader-ship giftedness and style

For more information see *www.yourjourney.org.*

6. Empowering Converts

The results of embracing, working, and reworking the first five micro principles will naturally lead to the empowering of your converts into leadership positions within and beyond your local church. When I work with church planters I routinely ask them these three questions:

Whom are you going after?

Whom are you attracting?

Whom are you investing in?

How they answer these questions often determines the future of their church. If they are going after the unchurched and yet attracting an overwhelming percentage of transfer growth, the church will drift from its mission. If they are attracting the unchurched and primarily investing in those leaders who have transferred from other churches, this will eventually distract the church from its disciple-making vision. When I visit churches, I frequently ask the lay leaders I meet how they came to be involved in their church. Rarely do I meet someone who has been a convert of that ministry who is now in the leadership of the church. I always wonder, "Where are the by-products of the church's vision? What happened to all the converts they had reached over the years? Why are they not being raised up to a leadership level in the church?"

If churches are going after and attracting the unchurched, then they need to invest in their converts by empowering them into leadership positions. Edwin Louis Cole has written one of the best definitions of spiritual maturity: "Maturity doesn't come with age, but begins with the acceptance of responsibility." I am convinced that someone who knows Jesus for three years can possess a higher level of spiritual maturity than someone who has been in the church for over 30 years. Maturity is an issue of obedience and responsibility, not an issue of longevity.

Every church planter needs to decide whom they are going to entrust with leadership. If they are unwilling to trust their converts in leadership roles, it really reveals that the church planters have a major obstacle to address in their own mind. If this is not dealt with, it will cause damage to their vision in one of two ways: (1) their converts will leave because they know they are not trusted or (2) the church will lose its conversion growth edge and will drift toward the national average of a mere one percent conversion growth rate annually.

The way church planters answer the question will determine how they maneuver around this landmine of enfolding people into their church. We are convinced that church planters need to have a vision and a process of turning the church over to their converts and not to disgruntled believers who move from church to church. Failure to empower converts will thwart the mission of disciple making in the church.

Not long ago I was at a congregational meeting in a new church. The planter was communicating how the church was moving toward installing formal leadership in the church. During that time he introduced three men whom he was recommending to the church as leaders. Each man communicated his vision for the church, his love for his pastor, and the honor they felt to be considered for leadership. One said these exact words: "I guess I am a product of this church, because three years ago I gave my life to Jesus through the ministry of this church, and I can't believe the amazing things God has done with my life since then."

What a powerful message that communicated throughout the whole church and to every convert. The message is that God is big enough not only to change a human heart, but he's also big enough to use, in a powerful way, those who are willing to accept the responsibility of leadership.

Questions to Ponder (While Standing in This Minefield)

When will we develop a ministry flowchart?

What can we do right now about first impressions?

What is our Second Touch Thermometer score? How will we improve?

What are some new Second Touch ideas?

Is there a particular modular training model that we will adopt?

LANDMINE 7:

FEAR OF MONEY

We make a living by what we get, we make a life by what we give.
Sir Winston Churchill

Money frees you from doing things you dislike.
Since I dislike doing nearly everything, money is handy.
Groucho Marx

In my earliest days of church planting, I was overwhelmed with the fact that I was actually receiving a salary and that we had a couple of thousand dollars in an account for expenses. Having just come out of seminary, I thought any amount of money seemed enormous. A good friend contacted me with an offer to support our venture financially. However, I couldn't think of how we could use his money, so I politely declined. I mentioned this to another church planting colleague not long after that, and his mouth fell open. "You what? You turned down money? Don't ever turn down money!"

I've learned a lot since then. Dwight Moody reportedly used to say, "The only money that's tainted is the money that 'tain't ours!" Wise church planters are always looking for ways to bring resources to the cause, but I'm afraid that not enough of us are wise. Fear of—or neglect of—money issues is another landmine that too often strangles our effectiveness. So let's talk about how to get past that fear or neglect so we can get Kingdom resources to our Kingdom projects.

The Roots of Fear and Neglect

In general I trace the fear or neglect of money issues to church planters' personal rejection issues, coupled with a skeptical society rampant with stories of financial abuse. When Gary was planting his church, networking with his community contacts, he talked with a real-estate agent. She said, "Boy, these are tough days for guys like you!" Gary asked her to clarify. She said, "With all of the televangelists and money scandals, these have got to be tough days for guys like you!"

Most church planters gravitate toward some level of seeker-sensitivity when they choose a model for their church. We believe that newcomers should feel safe, and we applaud the mantra that they should not be expected to "Say anything, sing anything, give anything." That much is fine. However, we waddle along without ever confronting the issue of finances until our vision is eclipsed by our resources — and the ministry is choked. I've been around many church planters, and my observation is that when many of them say, "I want to reach unchurched people" they really mean, "I want to reach unchurched people who already love Jesus and tithe"! I remember a cartoon in a Christian magazine that showed people shaking hands with the pastor as they were leaving church. As they leave they say, "Boy, Pastor, were we ever glad to hear you say that you didn't know where the money was coming from for the new building. For a minute there we thought that you thought it was coming from us!"

Of course, there are those few who truly don't need money. For some reason God has blessed them with enough of a financial base that they never have to lower themselves to bring up the money issue. But even these church planters don't yet understand stewardship. The basic educational principle that these church planters need to understand is that when it comes to teaching stewardship, It's not about how much the church needs; it's about what the Lord wants! Learn that as your new mantra, and you'll be halfway there.

What if I told you that you could teach stewardship faithfully, have all the money you'd need to conduct the ministry the way God wanted it—and in the process you would have people who were glad you did it—wouldn't you want to get into the game? Well, that's what I'm going to tell you. But first, you need to agree with three foundational issues.

The first issue I need to have compliance on is that **God blesses faithful stewards**. If you believe that's true, then you're in line with biblical teaching. Again and again the Bible reminds us that we have a responsibility to be good stewards, but in line with that responsibility comes the blessing of God. Before you were seeker-sensitive, you used to preach Malachi 3:10: "Test me in this," says the Lord Almighty, " and see if I will not throw open the floodgates of heaven and pour out so much blessing that you will not have room enough for it." Or Luke 6:38. "Give, and it will be given to you. A good measure, pressed down, shaken together and running over, will be poured into your lap. For with the measure you use, it will be measured to you." Or 2 Corinthians 9:11: "You will be made rich in every way so that you can be generous on every occasion, and through us your generosity will result in thanksgiving to God." In fact, I'll bet that you have dozens of stories of how God took care of you because you were faithful in your stewardship. So let's try to remember that God blesses those who are generous stewards. I once took a class from one of the great founders of the modern church growth movement, Dr. Peter Wagner. He said emphatically, "If you're not teaching your people to tithe, you're robbing them!"

The second foundation on which I need compliance was alluded to earlier. Your new mantra is to be: **It's not about what the church needs; it's about what the Lord wants!** Put that one on your doorpost, on your forehead, or wherever it can most likely be ground into your psyche. Let me explain. Too often leaders of new churches are focused narrowly on how much money they are bringing in. That's understandable. Bills need to be paid, and the early days of a church are fragile. The result is that church planters habitually focus on what it is that the church needs: Are we meeting budget? Are we meeting basic expenses? Very subtly we gauge victory or defeat on whether we're making budget. And if we're meeting budget, we think that we don't need to teach on stewardship.

Not only is that poor theology, but as in the case with any poor theology it will eventually come back to bite those who hold it. Sooner or later your vision will be outstripped by your lack of resources. Further, it may be that God has bigger dreams for your church than you do. If you had an abundance of money, you could change more lives for eternity. You're out to teach the whole counsel of God, and part of your responsibility is to create a stewardship culture that will permeate the church and give it the muscle to impact its world as it should.

Church planters should not be satisfied if they are making budget but their people are not being good stewards. And conversely, church planters should be satisfied when their people are being faithful stewards, even if the offerings are less than satisfactory. It's not about what the church needs; it's about what the Lord wants.

Third, I need you to agree that **it's O.K. to teach about tithing**. As I've told you, Gary and I have been around enough church planters to have heard every argument, pro and con, about tithing. Some believe that giving ten percent was abolished along with the other Old Testament laws with the coming of Christ. Some, citing 1 Corinthians 16:2, prefer "percentage giving," without mandating ten percent: "On the first day of every week, each one of you should set aside a sum of money in keeping with his income." To each objection to tithing, we respond by saying that one way or another, the tithe appears to be at least a minimum standard of stewardship throughout the Old and New Testaments.

Consider Jesus' teaching in Matthew 23:23. Addressing those who held strongly to the minutiae of the law, he said, "Woe to you, teachers of the law and Pharisees, you hypocrites! You give a tenth of your spices — mint, dill and cumin. But you have neglected the more important matters of the law — justice, mercy and faithfulness. You should have practiced the latter, without neglecting the former." I'm not looking for a theological argument here. I'll only observe that Jesus advocated that neglecting the tithe was wrong.

Ingredients to Creating a Stewardship Culture

Armed with these convictions, let's get specific about how to teach stewardship in a way that is both seeker-sensitive and effective in moving people toward obedience. And remember, we're seeking to create a stewardship culture in this church—an atmosphere where sacrificial giving of time, talent, and treasure is celebrated as the norm.

God's Guarantee Card

When Michael Gerber wrote his popular book *The E-Myth* (Harper Business, © 1995), he was teaching a basic principle: excellent systems that are run by average people can yield excellent results. In other words, when you have a proven way to bring about an action, go with it! I once heard Bill Bright talk about the early days of Campus Crusade for Christ. A business consultant told him that he needed a routine way to share the gospel. If he came up with something, it would increase the ministry's evangelistic performance substantially. Bright said he bristled at the idea at first because it seemed so "canned." But that led to the creation of the Four Spiritual Laws, scratched out in its initial form on a restaurant napkin. That canned mechanism has won millions to Christ.

In the world of stewardship training, one of my favorite mechanisms was popularized by John Maxwell, now of InJoy Ministries. Called "God's Guarantee Card," it is a basic commitment card committing signees to tithe for a period of ninety days. If, after the end of that period they think they've made a mistake, the church will refund what they've given. In my early days of church planting, Bob Logan of CoachNet encouraged me to try the God's Guarantee Card, saying that offerings in a new church generally go up 40 to 60 percent, and they stay up because people's lives are blessed. I did a four-week sermon series, culminating with God's Guarantee Card, and offerings did go up and stay up by 60 percent almost immediately. Besides that, I kept hearing stories of changed lives because people were willing to trust God in their stewardship.

I think that the key advantage to using this type of tool is that you are actually moving people to a commitment. As leaders we are often called to move beyond hinting and encouraging; we're called to bring people to make a change. The card provides opportunity for commitment, and it serves as a tracking tool to serve someone who might actually want their money back, which is very unlikely.

The God's Guarantee Card can be delivered in countless environments. The obvious one is in the context of an annual sermon series on stewardship. The card is delivered on the last or next-to-last Sunday of the series. And it can be done in a seeker-sensitive fashion. The generous use of humor, drama, and testimony helps soften the stereotype that this church only exists to get attendees' money. It's wise throughout the ninety-day testing period to remind

---

God's Guarantee Card

"Bring the whole tithe into the storehouse, that there may be food in my house. Test me in this," says the Lord Almighty, "and see if I will not throw open the floodgates of heaven and pour out so much blessing that you will not have room enough for it." (Malachi 3:10)

My part: By God's grace I will contribute 10 percent of my income for the next 90 days to Community Church.

God's part: To bless me according to Malachi 3:10.

Community Church's part: If at the end of 90 days I feel that tithing has been a mistake, has not resulted in the blessing of God, or has created a financial hardship, Community Church will refund me all that has been contributed during that period of time.

_____   _____
                    Signature   Date

Printed Name: _____

Phone Number: _____

---

people that the commitment expires on a certain date, and it's also wise to have those whose lives are being blessed through tithing to get a chance to tell their story. That can happen during a service, as an interview, or in a written testimony in a newsletter or bulletin. We recommend doing this on an annual basis, with January being the preferred month, to coincide with the new calendar and fiscal year.

Besides the public worship service, I recommend using the card in other contexts. Use it in membership classes and in discipleship relationships. Challenge early leaders to sign up and try it—to see if God does what he's promised. If you make it part of your repertoire, it will play an important part in developing a stewardship culture in your church.

When producing the God's Guarantee Card, it's best to have a duplicate made, so each participant has a copy of their commitment and the church treasurer does as well. That way the church actually does have a record of those who are eligible should they want their money back. Many churches create the above example in duplicate form with a perforation between the copies to enhance the ease of the commitment.

The Offering Box versus The Collection

What about the offering that is collected during the worship service? This can be a great time of modeling and genuine worship. However, it is not unusual these days for some new churches to prefer an offering box that attendees can visit if they wish. I don't have a problem with that if it does in fact produce stewards. "It's not what the church needs; it's what the Lord wants." Some church planters are so subtle about the existence of the offering box that they are sacrificing both money and modeling.

Using the offering box can be all right. However, you still need to teach and model stewardship to your people. And do remember this: it's always harder to tighten up than loosen up. If you go with the offering box and eventually need to change to receiving the offering during the service, expect the shrapnel to fly. Gary tells me that he once heard Bill Hybels say that one of his earliest regrets at Willow Creek Community Church was using an offering box rather than collecting the offering during the service. When they switched to taking an offering some time later, they ran into considerable opposition.

My own preference is to take a traditional offering, reminding those in attendance that this part of the service is for those who consider this their church home. I like the wording that experienced church planter Terry Martell in Green Bay, Wisconsin, uses. Each week at offering time he says, "We call this portion of our service 'love gifts.' We want to remember that our motivation for giving is love, not duty or compulsion or manipulation. We give freely as an act of worship. It's a gift. If you're a guest this morning, please don't feel under any obligation to give. We are interested in giving something to you, not getting something from you." Then Terry places his offering in the basket as the ushers start the collection. That's a great way to model the process, and it helps the congregation understand that their pastor is a steward, too.

Financial Seminars, Small Groups, and Discipleship

Many new churches have found success in hosting financial seminars, with topics particularly geared toward the young families that are being targeted by the church. Topics including real estate, insurance, wealth building from God's perspective, estate planning, and stewardship fit nicely into developing a stewardship culture. Often the church can staff this seminar with the people in the church, and frequently their denominational office will have some advisors to help as well. Or, by bringing in outsiders to help staff the event, additional bridges are built with the community.

Along the same line as the financial seminar, some small groups can be geared toward stewardship, a component of which is financial stewardship. And no discipleship process should exclude financial stewardship. Once again, you're doing your new converts a favor when you teach them to obey God in this area.

Bulletin and Newsletter Reminders

Ultimately, it's not about what the church needs, but it doesn't hurt for the members to know what the church needs, either. A whole host of newcomers to a church don't have a clue that somebody's paying the bills. They may assume that some higher-ups have this taken care of, but that's rarely the case (nor should it be!). And if such newcomers do give anything, it's usually low-level tipping, as if they are paying for services rendered. So I think it's a good idea to publish each week in the bulletin the amount collected the previous week (or the average over a few weeks) alongside of what is needed for the budget.

When I was pastoring a new church, I would also paste the following words next to the financial figures: "Your sacrifice to help the ministry of Community Church matters. But remember, it's not about what the church needs; it's about what the Lord wants." Also include some financial updates in the church newsletter. And one other hint: in a new church, always add the names of the parents and grandparents of members who visit the church and volunteer their addresses to your newsletter mailing list. They are usually quite happy that their children or grandchildren are actually going to church, and by cultivating this relationship you will be surprised how many of these long-distance friends begin to help financially.

Capital Campaigns

Capital campaigns are those every-once-in-a-while special-project fundraising efforts for things beyond the normal scope of the budget: purchasing land, building, debt retirement, or adding a new staff position. You're probably familiar with how these work. A chairman and leadership team are recruited, goals are agreed upon, mailing lists are devised, literature is produced, and it all culminates in a victory banquet of some sort. People are asked to make commitments for an over-and-above gift for two or three years. Usually a three-year program will bring somewhere between two thirds to one full year's worth of additional revenue into the church. (In other words, if your annual budget is $100,000, a three-year capital campaign will bring in an additional $67,000 to $100,000.)

The approach may be canned, but it shouldn't be overlooked. Unfortunately, too many church planters think that capital campaigns are for the older, established churches. But I disagree. I once heard my friend Terry Martell say to a group of church planters whom he was mentoring, "The time to have a capital campaign is two years before you think you'll need it!" Why would this be so?

There are several reasons to do capital campaigns sooner than later. First, in the early days of survival you won't have much of a stewardship culture in your church. Proportionally speaking, offerings will be lower than they should be. At the very least, capital campaigns generate more revenue.

Second, they create ownership of ministry. Virtually every one of these programs involves getting a large percentage of the congregation involved in one committee or another: publicity, hospitality, banquet arrangements, prayer, or visitation. Third, it helps legitimize the new church to its constituents and the broader community. A church that is already setting aside money for land, for instance, will be perceived as being here to stay.

There are various ways to form and get capital campaigns underway. At the casual end of the spectrum you could simply call everyone together for a special evening dessert, where the groundwork has been paved for a special financial commitment to be made. Toward the middle of the spectrum you can purchase a "campaign in a box" from various sources and essentially do the project on your own. That can also work.

However, generally speaking, both Gary and I believe that your need for professional help increases proportionately to the significance of the event. Get professional help from one of many solid stewardship ministries out there. Yes, you'll pay for their services. But the payoff will be significant, not only in terms of dollars raised, but also in terms of avoiding huge mistakes that can be anticipated only by experienced personnel. Ask yourself this question: If a big-time operation such as Willow Creek Community Church in South Barrington, Illinois, seeks professional help when they do a capital funds campaign, shouldn't we? If any church should have the talent to pull off a campaign on their own, Willow Creek should. And maybe they do have the talent, but they've learned the value of getting professional help.

Finally, Seeker Sensitivity

Now that I've got you all nervous about money, let me calm you down with some final reminders that it's very possible to teach stewardship without being labeled as money-hungry. In all likelihood, you're planting a church that is to some degree sensitive to the unchurched pre-Christian who is in your church. You craft your language to avoid baffling Unchurched Harry and Mary. And maybe you even pride yourself on laying low on the money issue. As a matter of fact, I think you can have so much fun creating a stewardship culture in your church that with a little innovation you can be as seeker-sensitive or seeker-driven as you want.

I know this from experience. When I was a rookie church planter, I got an idea from Bob Logan that I built upon for my first stewardship sermon. Someone interrupted me during the introduction of the sermon by standing up and shouting, "I knew it! I knew it! I come to church for the first time in twenty years and all they want is my money!" The interrupter was dressed in a loud plaid suit with a striped tie, and he wore a rumpled old men's hat. I immediately began a dialog with him, and invited him to come up front. In our conversation he told me that he was a vacuum cleaner salesman passing through town. He had seen our ad, so he came to church. In fact, he pulled a vacuum cleaner out of his suitcase as he spoke. By now the crowd was up for grabs, having detected that this was a setup. The man and I talked about the money issue, and I asked him to sit down to give me a chance to explain. I then addressed the crowd, "Some of you are feeling just like our friend Hank." It was a great way to defuse the tension, add some humor, and set up a great teaching environment.

Another time I did a stream-of-consciousness sermon. My audio crew helped me record it ahead of time with reverb, to mimic the notion that listeners were hearing my thoughts. We played that prerecorded tape during the sermon time, where we had the stage set up as my office. I walked in, did my biblical exegesis, prepared my sermon about giving, and went through the motions. While the congregation watched and listened to me create my sermon, they heard me struggle. "God, please help my people realize that you will bless them when they sacrifice. I don't want this to appear that this is a church that's greedy for their money. It's really not about what the church needs; it's about what you want."

Also, using God's Guarantee Card can be highly effective. When explained properly and in a seeker-sensitive fashion, the payoff can be huge. I've seen this successfully used many times, but one story topped them all. A new seeker-driven church in Mansfield, Ohio, introduced the God's Guarantee Card in its regular weekend seeker service. They utilized some of the plethora of great dramas available to humorously and seriously touch this issue. It was such a hit that the Guarantee Card appeared on the front page of the local newspaper, heralding the fact that this new church was innovative and upbeat in bringing up the money issue.

Get your creative people together and come up with a way to keep your seeker sensitivity while building that stewardship culture. Don't allow the landmine of money to take you out of the game of doing what God has called you to do.

Questions to Ponder (While Standing in This Minefield)

Have I been afraid to train people in stewardship? Why?

Do I truly believe that God blesses generosity?

Will I use the God's Guarantee Card?

When will we begin a capital funds campaign? What steps can we take right now?

Can we sponsor a financial seminar? What elements will we include?

LANDMINE 8:

UNDERESTIMATING SPIRITUAL WARFARE

The art of war is simple enough. Find out where your enemy is.
Get at him as soon as you can.
Strike him as hard as you can, and keep moving.
Ulysses S. Grant

War is not nice.
Barbara Bush

You may know that prayer is not preparation for the battle; prayer is the battle. But I'm not sure you believe it. And if you don't believe it, you'll step on Landmine eight: underestimating the degree of spiritual warfare levied against you and your new church. I came to understand this firsthand as a young church planter in Whitewater, Wisconsin.

When I first arrived in Whitewater, I wondered why there was no middle-of-the road evangelical church that was doing any relevant ministry to reach unbelievers with the gospel. We set up shop in a small office — in a renovated house that had become rundown and was subsequently turned into office space — and got to work.

I had heard that Whitewater had a storied past, related to the occult. In the little amount of research I did, I learned that at the beginning of the twentieth century a local resident named Morris Pratt had given himself over to Spiritism because he had made large sums of money on an iron ore mine investment on a tip from a spiritist medium. As a result he created the Morris Pratt Institute, which became America's largest school of Spiritism. A large, three-story building was built, and within a short time six full-time faculty and up to 45 students at a time were engaged in the training of occultism. Seances and the like took place every Sunday night on the third floor, and old-timers still refer to the building today as "Spook's Temple." The institute lasted for about twenty years.

Our ministry moved forward quite well. We did various things related to spiritual warfare. Many of our members were reading Frank Peretti's popular spiritual warfare novel *This Present Darkness* (Crossway, © 1986). We had regular nights of prayer and prayer meetings. And I, perhaps because I was so afraid of failure, would spend at least two hours each week on my knees in my little office asking for God's help in the work. Five years down the road we had completed construction on our first church building and had vacated the office space we had used during that time. As a thank-you gesture, my secretary and I took the other building tenants out for lunch. Over lunch there was a serious discussion about other building tenants having seen ghosts in the office building from time to time. One woman told me that the most dramatic time occurred the previous Halloween, when one ghost ("a short, Amish-dressed, white-bearded man") had tried to get into my office — but couldn't. These accounts were quite intriguing to my secretary and me. During the discussion, suddenly everything made sense when it was revealed that the office building we shared — the renovated house — was built around the turn of the century...by Morris Pratt. My office had been his living room! When I learned this, shivers went down my spine.

All of this is to say that I learned with first hand evidence that Ephesians 6:12 accurately reflects our world—we wage war against unseen evil forces. I know that my experiences are not unique, but they do help me to frame my suspicions about the whole of church planting. If spiritual dynamics were an important component of the church I planted in a small, seemingly insignificant town, it follows that there is spiritual opposition in any neglected community in our world—urban, suburan, small town, or rural. When we ask the question "Why isn't there a good church here?" or "Why isn't this group of people being reached?" part of the answer could be that forces of evil have prevented it so far.

Let's begin with the conviction that those involved in church planting need to do so with a biblical worldview, having a healthy respect for the unseen world. C. S. Lewis, in his introduction to *The Screwtape Letters* (Collier, © 1982), says, "There are two equal and opposite errors into which our race can fall about the devils. One is to disbelieve in their existence. The other is to believe, and to feel an excessive and unhealthy interest in them." There is a balance, to be sure, but whatever the case, we need to assume that there will be much hard work ahead. Church planting lore is replete with stories of Satan operating intention-ally to prevent the advance of the Kingdom of God. We've heard dozens of stories of demonic appearances, physical attack, diseases, sleeplessness, and so on. One church planter told me that his automobile suddenly died on the freeway late one night just as he told his driving companion that his sermon the following day was on spiritual warfare. Another told of his pet dog's agitation and refusal to enter his study one evening while he worked on his "spiritual warfare" sermon. Indications of spiritual warfare are numerous. But we're mistaken if we think that simple acknowledgement of spiritual warfare means we can let down our guard. George Otis, of the Sentinel Group, puts it this way:

> Spiritual warfare is hard work. It requires us to roll up our sleeves and slog it out. No magic wands. I'm distressed when I hear people talking as if there were some sort of magic wand, as if you could go into one of these areas which for century after century, thousands upon millions of people have used their own free-will choice to welcome demonic powers and principalities to live amongst them and rule over them. Don't tell me we're going to send in a little prayerwalk team to set aside the logical consequences of their free-will choices, pulling up centuries of demonic entrenchment just because we quote a verse or sing a good worship chorus. I'm sorry. It just doesn't work that way. There are no magic wands. But the effectual fervent prayer of righteous men and women avails much. If that verse (James 5:16) were not in Scripture, you and I would be in a bad way today. Fear might have a place in our midst. The next verse makes a point to say that wonder-working Elijah had no magic wand at all. He had a nature like ours." He simply prayed "earnestly." (*Prayerwalking*, Hawthorne and Kendrick, © 1993, pp. 134-35).

Gary and I have been around church planters most of our adult lives, and we've lived in that world ourselves. And as we've tried to get a handle on spiritual warfare as it is levied against church planters and their new churches, we've observed that most of it can be placed into one of three categories: discouragement, distractions, or disqualifications. Let's break these down and discuss strategies to win the war.

Discouragement

Humanly speaking, one of the easiest things to do is to dampen someone else's spirits. One properly timed criticism, threat, rumor, or innuendo can do incredible damage to a ministry and launch leaders into seasons of discouragement and even despair. The devil will exploit any opportunity to set you back, and we're "not unaware of his schemes" (1 Cor. 2:11). He will try to discourage you, and discouragement for church planters comes in many forms.

Sin in the Camp

The Bible tells of specific instances when sin got in the way of victory. One classic example is the story of Achan, found in Joshua 7. Israel was routed by the enemy, and Joshua couldn't understand why. He calls out to the Lord, "O Lord, what can I say, now that Israel has been routed by its enemies? The Canaanites and the other people of the country will hear about this and they will surround us and…" (v. 8). God informs Joshua that someone's disobedience had brought judgment, and he leads him on a systematic search for the perpetrator. Achan was the one; he had covertly and disobediently kept part of the plunder in an earlier battle. Joshua rebuked him and carried out the sentence, resulting in God's favor again. "Why have you brought this trouble on us? The Lord will bring trouble on you today. Then all of Israel stoned him…. Then the Lord turned from his fierce anger" (vv. 25-26).

Sound familiar? It is to a lot of church planters who wouldn't have minded stoning a person or two, either! In the early days of Gary's church plant, there was a season of nongrowth, frustration, and discouragement. I was Gary's coach, and we could not figure out why the project was not progressing, until "sin in the camp" was discovered. A key leader (someone I had recruited for Gary) had been pilfering a significant amount from the church's meager offerings. When we discovered what had happened, Gary and I gathered in the church office, got down on our knees, and prayed for God's mercy as we laid hands on the little file box that held the church's financial records. The sin was dealt with (without stoning), and genuine repentance was achieved, including eventual restoration to the church.

It would seem, too, that God has a particular jealousy of new ventures that are designed to bring glory to himself. In the early days of the church (Acts 5:1-11) Ananias and Sapphira paid with their lives, too, as a judgment against their sins of deception and cover-up. The result? "Great fear seized the whole church and all who heard about these events" (v. 11). At least in this case the judgment eventually resulted in a healthier church.

However, that's not always the case; and sometimes the works of the devil do, in fact, work. Our family was involved as laypeople in a new church plant that was having limited success. It was hard to put a finger on the reasons for the lack of growth. Eventually the pastor confessed to a recent history of homosexual activity. In this case the entire church plant eventually closed down. Those who lead new church plants should keep their eyes open, observing whether there may be sin in the camp. But they should also be aware that the evil one can orchestrate and exploit such situations.

Physical Hardship

I suppose we would need to do a true factor analysis to find out if there is more physical hardship among new church planters than in the general population of those who minister. But even without statistical verification, we can at least testify to the rampant way in which the powers of darkness wage war against our physical bodies and our physical world. I've seen numerous instances of young, healthy church planters spending inordinate amounts of time in doctor's offices and hospitals. Another story comes from the earlier days of Gary's church plant. Countryside Community Church was in the midst of building its launch team, working toward the day that the church would hold regular public services. Gary's wife, Mary, became afflicted with strep throat — six times in six months! — and was scheduled to have surgery at the worst possible time. Gary tells the bizarre way in which the Lord revealed to them that this was an attack from the enemy:

> During the daytime, before our Wednesday night prayer meeting, we received a letter from a missionary I had only met once. The letter recounted the story of his wife having had strep throat five times. The elders of church finally recognized it as an attack from Satan and prayed against it accordingly. She was marvelously healed. That night I read the letter to my young church and we prayed for Mary, identifying this as an attack from the evil one. Mary went to a presurgical check up at the doctor's office a few days later. The doctor looked at her throat and asked her, "Is this surgery going to be an inconvenience to you at this time?" Mary replied, "Yes!" The doctor said, "Well, your throat looks one hundred percent better. Let's put the surgery off for now." The next Wednesday we had twenty-nine people meeting in a launch team in our living room, praising God for winning the victory. And Mary was upstairs in our bedroom. No, she wasn't sick. She was teaching the launch team children about the mercy of God! That was fourteen years ago, and Mary has never had strep throat again.

Physical hardship as an attack from the enemy can go beyond bodily harm, of course. One of the finest church planters and church planting coaches I know, Bob Marsh (Gateway Community Church, Mayville, Wisconsin), saw so many mechanical attacks on their lives that they had to believe that it wasn't simply circumstantial. When the washing machine, dryer, lawnmower, and two automobiles all went out of commission in the span of a few weeks, they suspected they were being targeted.

The unseen world is real, and that unseen world interacts with the physical, seen world. Don't make the mistake of chalking up to circumstance each instance of physical hardship. It isn't wise or prudent to consider every difficulty as directed by the prince of darkness, but it is wise to observe patterns and be aware that the unseen world is as real as the physical one we operate it. We're not always ignorant of the devil's schemes.

Emotional Hardship

Following is a pattern I've observed. The first time I have meaningful contact with new church planters after they've been on the field for a while, I ask, "How's it going?" I often hear the response, "Well, it's really hard around here." The planters are saying that this particular location is more difficult than the other locations they had read about in the books—the locations they thought they were coming to. Yes, it is hard, but perhaps not uniquely so. Yes, certain places have powerful strongholds to overcome, and we should be aware of that. Church planting is a challenge, even when it's going well. And accordingly it makes sense that Satan would target our emotional well-being when we seek to assault the gates of hell. Emotionally, those who are involved in church planting can be targeted in numerous ways: fear, depression, worry, criticism, competitiveness, and jealousy.

To be sure, part of emotional hardship is simple immaturity that we need to overcome. I'm amazed at myself when I look back fifteen years and read some of my pathetic thinking in my journals, for example crying out to God with self-flagellation because that week's attendance was down 2 percent from the previous week's attendance. I was very immature, and Dave Mobley made a suggestion to help me. He said, "Why not ignore attendance figures until Thursday? That way you'll only have a couple of days each week to beat yourself up!" That helped, but it certainly exposed my weakness. Satan knows how to attack and exploit our weaknesses.

Fear

One subset of discouragement is fear. On numerous occasions I have made a statement in public that always draws head nods from those involved in starting new churches: "I think the most predominant emotion that new church planters have to battle is fear." Perhaps that's not a function of church planting as much as it's a function of immaturity. And since many church planters are young, their age and corresponding immaturity become a breeding ground for fear and an area that the enemy can easily exploit. There is very little perspective when difficulties come; every difficulty is perceived to be a crisis, so it's not unfathomable to consider that the father of lies is willing to exploit this.

As a young church planter, I was part of a group with three other pastors who gathered monthly just to listen to each other. I'm sure that a lot of the things I talked about had to do with the fragility of the church I was planting. (In reality, what I talked about probably had more to do with the fragility of my life!) One of my colleagues, an experienced pastor in a neighboring community, said something in passing that affected me: "You'll be surprised at the resiliency of God's church." I probably didn't believe him then, but over time that's become one of the axioms of my ministry and worldview.

Derailment

Derailment refers to those episodes of failure in the lives of leaders that have the potential to bring the ministry to a screeching halt. The Apostle Paul writes of his own effort to finish the course well: "No, I beat my body and make it my slave so that after I have preached to others, I myself will not be disqualified for the prize" (1 Cor. 9:27). Unfortunately, I've seen enough of that, too. Several years ago our family was part of a new church plant in our community that, after a slow start, had really picked up momentum. Just when it was going well, the church planter came to me and confessed his sin of homosexual behavior and adultery. It was certainly a struggle for this man, and over the course of time he yielded to the temptation and ended up being disqualified. Not surprisingly, that church is no longer in existence.

In church planting we're shooting with real bullets. This stuff really matters, and since the prize is so critical, it's important to understand that leaders in new church ventures will be targeted for derailment. I devote chapter one, on personal health and growth, to this very topic.

For now, let's agree that part of the enemy's strategy is to derail effective leaders. And part of our strategy is to fight vigorously. A good friend of mine recently had a mild heart attack. He was overweight and out of shape. During his recovery phase his cardiologist gave him a wake-up call. He said, "Heart attack victims are notorious for changing their life patterns—short-term. But within a year of recovery, only 17 percent have continued their regimen of diet and exercise." My friend is asking countless people to keep him accountable to being among the 17 percent. He's being strategic in winning the battle over his health.

Counterattack: The God-Dependent Church

It disheartens me when I see some new churches—especially those in years two to ten — act as though they can get by with their excellent programming and sociological acumen. I'm all for excellent programming and sociological acumen, but not to the neglect of spiritual empowerment. Some of these new churches were extremely God-dependent in their prenatal (before launch) phase. Leaders begged and pleaded with the Lord to make this thing work. And he answered! But when regular services started happening and the church looked as if it would survive, spiritual dependence on God began to slip, too.

When new churches neglect their spiritual empowerment, they are shunning the greatest strength they have. I want to challenge these churches to remember that they have great power to see their ministries thrive—if they depend on God.

The story of Jehoshaphat in 2 Chronicles 20 is a classic example of reliance on God in the midst of attack. His prayer reminds us that ultimately, as leaders, we must bring our lives, our people, and our ministries into utter dependence on God. "But now here are men from Ammon, Moab and Mount Seir, whose territory you would not allow Israel to invade when they came from Egypt; so they turned away from them and did not destroy them. See how they are repaying us by coming to drive us out of the possession you gave us as an inheritance. O our God, will you not judge them? For we have no power to face this vast army that is attacking us. We do not know what to do, but our eyes are upon you" (2 Chron. 20:10-12).

Of course, according to the text, God wins the day. "All the men of Judah, with their wives and children and little ones, stood there before the Lord . Then the Spirit of the Lord came upon Jahaziel... as he stood in the assembly. He said: 'Listen, King Jehoshaphat and all who live in Judah and Jerusalem! This is what the Lord says to you: "Do not be afraid or discouraged because of this vast army." ' "

In our hearts, we know this is true. Blessed are we if we do something about it. In case you need more motivation, let me conclude this section with a fascinating story reported by George Otis, an event that occurred in Algeria in the early 1980s. One evening, in the sovereignty of God, each person in a Muslim coastal village of 500 received the same dream —that Jesus Christ was Lord. The following day the place was abuzz with discussion, and over the following few weeks all the villagers placed their faith in the lordship of Jesus. Missionaries who did follow-up work were perplexed that such an event could or would take place. George Otis tells what happened:

> It was at virtually this very site that, in June 1315, Raymond Lull, a Spanish missionary from Majorca, had been stoned to death by frenzied Muslims after preaching in the open market. The blood of martyrs, it has often been said, represents the seed of the Church. Lull, who is generally considered to be the first missionary to the Muslims, certainly believed this. In his book, *The Tree of Life*, he wrote that Islamic strongholds are best conquered "by love and prayers, and the pouring out of tears and blood." In retrospect, it appears that it was precisely this formula that summoned the recent supernatural events in Algeria. Falling into the ground on that summer day in the fourteenth century, the seed of Raymond Lull's poured-out life was subsequently watered by the tears of genera-tions of pious intercessors. (*The Last of the Giants*, Chosen Books, © 1991, pp. 157-58).

As those involved in starting new churches, we will do well to pray and pray and pray. We will do well to teach our church to pray and pray and pray. We will not make the mistake of seeing the church as a mere sociological entity; we will see it as a living organism, entirely dependent on the one who claims to build his church. We are under attack, but the gates of hell will not prevail.

Ideas for Creating a God-Dependent Church

If our objective is to become God-dependent, what are some specific ways to bring that about? There are certainly dozens and dozens of ideas. Here are just a few.

Creating a Culture of Dependence

To begin, I think it's a good idea to set the tone from start to finish that this is a church that truly needs God. The pastor can communicate that through sermons and personal life anecdotes. Testimonies can be given routinely by people who know what it is to trust God. All the people who take the microphone during a worship service can be coached to craft their thinking and words to reflect a culture of dependence. Certainly I'm not suggesting false humility or self-degradation; we all know what true humility looks like and how that can be such a powerful communicator.

Intercession Teams

I think that, in general, most churches consider themselves to be God-dependent. That's especially true of new churches and their leaders during those scary first days. When we first planted our church, I was scared enough to hand-write postcards each Monday to send out to a group of about twenty intercessors around the state so they could be praying. Scared can be good. But when fear subsides, sometimes our God-dependence does too. As a matter of fact, after our new church got up and running and appeared to be for real, I foolishly phased out my intercession team.

God-dependency for a new church begins with God-dependency in the church planter. I eventually formed another intercession team that attempts to pray for me daily; I have maintained that team ever since. I recruit people who evidence that they are people of prayer, and I have a wide array of intercessors. They receive routine communiqués from me (usually monthly, via email), and they sign on until the first of the year. Then they can renew their commitment until the following year. One bit of administrative advice: when you recruit new intercessors, don't ask them to sign on for a year; ask them to sign on until a specific date when everyone renews. That will save you the hassle of trying to figure out when it was that so-and-so joined the team.

Specialized Prayer Teams

It's easy enough for a new church to become more self-dependent than God-dependent. In my years as a church planting pastor I was forced to push our church toward God-dependency. Usually the factor that nudged me in that direction was a falling monthly attendance in comparison to the previous year. Each time that happened, I called the church to prayer, and attendance increased again. We would have a 6:00 a.m. prayer meeting that did not take prayer requests. We would start praying by 6:05, and the conditions of the meeting were that participants could pray for (1) growing church attendance, (2) conversions, and (3) hurting people. We would conclude by 6:45. It was perhaps the best investment of time our young church had.

Fasting

Yes, you can get a new church to fast. With proper instruction many will enjoin the Lord in this way, deepening their walk with God and creating a sense of true dependence. Times of fasting can be called when there are major decisions to be made or when there are crises that need a focused attention.

I recently learned of a variation on fasting from Pastor Melvin Hargrove of the urban Zoe Outreach Ministries in Racine, Wisconsin. On occasion Pastor Hargrove calls the leaders of his church to a "Daniel fast." Referring to the Old Testament hero, a Daniel fast involves abstinence from meat, snacks, and sweets. In general, it's a fruit-and-vegetable fast. Like any fast it places the leaders in a frame of dependence and reminds them to entreat the Lord.

Specialized Prayer Meetings

Churchwide specialized prayer meetings can also put the church in a position of dependence upon God. Some of the best-attended special events in the seeker-sensitive church that I planted were our full nights and half nights of prayer. It was normal to see God move in powerful ways. A few years into the church plant we noticed that there was no one from the northwest corner of our small community who was actively involved in our church. In concert with a direct-mail campaign advertising a new sermon series, we hosted a half night of prayer that culminated with a prayer drive (a mechanical version of a prayer walk) in the part of town that was most unreached. That following Sunday we had five families visit, and three of those families ended up assimilating into the body of the church.

Prayers for Healing

The Bible does call us to pray for healing, but many evangelicals, and especially those in seeker-sensitive or seeker-driven churches do little about that. My theology is not specifically charismatic or Pentecostal, so my journey to pray for physical healing was a slow and steady one. When I finally developed a balanced understanding of this issue (one that neither over-promised or under-promised results), we began to routinely pray for peoples' physical needs in public settings. In our case we would offer occasional prayer meetings for healing—usually every month or so—when people could come to the church and have the elders pray over them. We saw many maladies cured, both of a physical and emotional nature. By placing ourselves in a position of need before the Lord, we were able to experience blessing as a church. Jesus said, "The thief kills, steals and destroys, but I came that they might have life and have it to the full" (John 10:10). Such dependence on God surely engages the enemy in spiritual warfare.

The Individual Prayer Life of the Leader

Writes Thomas White:

> In the same sense that a secret agent sends out a signal that merits serious attention by the opposition, so the Christian walking in obedience to the Spirit of God, abiding in prayer, and committed to the kingdom stirs enemy opposition. The stakes are higher for the veteran who can do the most damage to the domain of darkness. My premise should be clear by now: any servant of Jesus Christ who poses a serious threat to the powers of hell will be targeted and will encounter resistance, especially at times of strategic ministry. The anointed agent of Christ's kingdom must be equipped to discern and deal with the efforts of the enemy's kingdom. (*Engaging the Enemy*, pp. 65-66).

While it is necessary for those engaged in church planting to have others around them committed to intercession, we would be remiss to ignore the fact that it's necessary that individual leaders of new church plants have at least a semblance of spiritual discipline and vitality as well. For new churches, it's obvious that key leaders will be targets of satanic/demonic attack, and a weak spiritual core of the leader could spell disaster for other players in the movement. George Otis puts the prayer habits of many Christian leaders into perspective:

> Although prayer is routinely acknowledged as an important component of global evangelization efforts, these expressions are more often the product of religious habit than they are of any genuine conviction. Like other religious peoples around the world, we pray because we are hesitant to embark on significant undertakings without first acknowledging (God). Any specific requests is of less importance than insuring we have not caused offense by neglecting to inform Him of our intentions. In this sense, prayer is more superstitious and prophylactic than it is supernatural and procreative. (*Breaking Strongholds in Your City*, Regal, © 1993, p. 18)

There seems to be at least a correlational (if not causational!) linkage between the spiritual vitality of a leader and the blessing of God on the movement. (To be sure, however, the grace of God has mercifully covered many church planting efforts where the spiritual vitality of the leader was weak.) The admonition of Paul Yonggi Cho, founding pastor of Yoido Full Gospel Church in Seoul, South Korea, is notable:

It is also necessary for those who are called to engage in this spiritual warfare to be holy and sanctified, because He is a holy God. Many who have cast out demons, who have prophesied, and who have done wonders in His Name may find God declaring, "Depart from me you who practice lawlessness, I never knew you." The devil has crept into the church and promoted iniquity, lawlessness, and unrighteousness in our midst.

It breaks my heart to see so many co-workers for the Kingdom falling in disgrace. Like the seven sons of Sceva, the evil spirit has lept upon them, overpowered them, prevailed against them, and they fled out of their homes naked and wounded. Without holiness and sanctification, without great sacrifice, and without a fervent prayer life, many will be so wounded. The evil spirit will answer, "Jesus I know, Paul I know, but who are you?" (*Engaging the Enemy*, p. 119)

The frenetic lives of the leaders of a new church work against a disciplined prayer life. Nevertheless, it is crucial to make the time for regular prayer. "But Jesus often withdrew to lonely places and prayed" (Luke 5:16); we should as well. Though each leader will choose his or her own course, some components of a spiritually vital life might include:

Having a daily time for prayer

Reading through the Bible annually

Taking a monthly retreat day

Having a spiritual mentor or mentors, with some sort of accountability

Traveling, when possible, with spiritually mature friends

Fasting on a regular basis

Joining someone else's intercessor team

Keeping a prayer list

Having "historical mentors" and carrying their writings with you

Reading biographies of great men and women of faith

I am a pragmatist at heart, and I do not discuss spiritual warfare simply because it is the expected thing to do. We who love God's church may miss some deep and fruitful blessing because we have not yet gone deep with him. Deepening our relationship with him can help us avoid the landmine of underestimating spiritual warfare.

Be self-controlled and alert. Your enemy the devil prowls around like a roaring lion looking for someone to devour. Resist him, standing firm in the faith because you know that your brothers throughout the world are undergoing the same kind of sufferings. And the God of all grace, who called you into his eternal glory in Christ, after you have suffered a little while, will himself restore you and make you strong, firm and steadfast. To him be the power for ever and ever. Amen. (1 Peter 5: 8-11).

Questions to Ponder (While Standing in This Minefield)

How have I minimized spiritual warfare in this new church?

Looking back, where have we seen attacks from the enemy?

How will we call our church to God-dependence?

Where do I need to increase my God-dependence? How?

Who will hold me accountable?

LANDMINE 9:

MISFIRING ON HIRING

Like an archer who wounds at random is he who hires a fool or any passer-by.
Proverbs 26:10

Making a mistake on hiring your first staff creates a potentially explosive situation. That your church has grown to the level of hiring additional staff is a tremendous feat in itself. But it can be crushing if that first hire is a bad one. Think of all the people wounded by a bad hire: the staff person, those under the care of the staff person, the family of the staff person, other leaders, and you. For example, the staff person overseeing our music ministry was unwilling to confront a drummer who habitually played too loud. Then, during one of our worship services, a most unnerving event took place. A relatively new attender stood up, walked up to the drummer, and told him that he was playing too loud. That demoralizing event sticks in my mind when I think of the wounds that can be caused by a bad hire. It was the beginning of the end for the staff person, and the drummer eventually drifted away.

Getting the right people in your organization will determine the level of success that you will see. And yet, so often we see significant difficulties when a new church hires its first staff. In theory, it will reduce the workload for the pastor/church planter. In practice, it often brings utter frustration. If there ever was an "antipersonnel" landmine, this is it. So many people are hurt when we misfire in our hiring. Below are some suggestions on navigating the hiring landmines in a new church.

Understand the Owner Employee Tension

In most entrepreneurial ventures there is a tension between owners and employees. If you ask any solo business owner who is working about ninety hours a week what their biggest hiring fear is, you'll hear, "Will the person I hire care as much about the business as I do?" (Eric Wahlgren, *"The First*

Employee," Inc. Magazine, February 2004, p. 30) Church planters live with this same concern because they have sacrificed tremendously to see this new church started. They have often left the safety of a secure position; they have raised financial support; they have endured loneliness and rejection. They have tirelessly worked at gathering people around a common vision. They have launched the church and have built it to the point where they have created enough resources to employ more people.

Church planters see themselves as owners — not as employees. And therein lies the tension. In most cases it will take years before any new staff hires will feel a sense of true ownership. And it's very unlikely that the staff person will ever feel the full ownership intensity of the founding church planter. This begs two questions: (1) Is it possible to find staff people with the same level of ownership as the planter? And (2) How can this level of ownership be developed?

Is it possible to find staff people with the same level of ownership as the planter? Yes, from the ministry partners with whom you started the church. Planter Joe Basile, in Lombard, Illinois, has three volunteer staff working right now in his new church. These are friends and family who left everything to see the dream of a new church become a reality. Each has displayed the same level of commitment as Joe, and they've worked tirelessly to see it succeed. The quandary that Joe will face is which one to hire first when monies are available.

Deep levels of ownership can also be found among your volunteers. Every pastor knows the difference between those who are doing time in a ministry and those who are passionately committed to the task at hand. Sometimes all it takes is a little training and skill development to make a volunteer into an exceptional staff person. There are dozens and dozens of examples of volunteers eventually becoming tremendous staff members. But there is one liability. Keep in mind that it's harder to fire a person from within, especially if your church is in a small community. There is no easy way for them to move on.

How can this level of ownership be developed? By building trust and showing appreciation. When employees feel trusted and deeply appreciated for their contributions, their level of ownership increases. Conversely, when a staff person senses nothing but suspicion and criticism, the level of ownership dissipates very quickly. Properly resourcing and equipping staff members so they can do their work with excellence also helps secure loyalty. Tim Stevens and Tony Morgan offer the following advice:

> Everyone's expected to do more with less – more ministry with less staff, more ministry with less money, and more ministry with less time. One way to deal with this reality is to make sure your team is properly equipped with the latest gadgets to encourage multitasking. I have no way to measure it, but I really believe I give more time to ministry and accomplish far more because I have the right

tools at my finger tips. Is it twice as much? I don't know, but it's significant, and it's a relatively cheap return on the investment when you consider the cost of salary and benefits that it would take to replace my time. (*Simply Strategic Stuff*, Group Publishing, ©2003, p. 30)

A well-equipped staff is an encouraged staff. Someone has said, "If you need a piece of equipment but don't already have it, you're already paying for it." Along with providing equipment, it is also essential to resource your staff with strategic conferences, educational opportunities, and an adequate budget to perform their ministry. This is a major attitude change for most church planters. They were the ones who scraped and clawed their church's way into existence. They watched every penny and felt personal pain with every damaged microphone cord. And now they are asked to equip others with a proper budget. But without this strategic change, the result will be discouraged and frustrated employees who will never achieve the level of ownership that is desired.

The Youth Pastor Mistake and the Shepherd-Equipper Tension

There is nothing that can institutionalize your new church more than hiring a full-time youth pastor. Making your first staff addition a full-time youth pastor reinforces the idea that only professionals can do ministry rather than the idea of viewing staff as being equippers of ministry. It's a natural and unquestioned progression for church members to assume that a youth pastor would be the next hire. "After all," they reason, "we already have a pastor for the adults."

Yet this mindset is what can cause a church to plateau instead of reaching its growth potential. This is the shepherd-equipper tension. Laypeople press that we hire pastors to care for the sheep. No one would argue that pastors are to provide shepherding care for God's flock, but there is another role that must be prioritized. Pastors are also to be "equippers of the saints." The Apostle Paul addressed this issue in his letter to the church in Ephesus:

It was he who gave some to be apostles, some to be prophets, some to be evangelists, and some to be pastors and teachers, *to prepare God's people for works of service, so that the body of Christ may be built up* until we all reach unity in the faith and in the knowledge of the Son of God and become mature, attaining to the whole measure of the fullness of Christ. (Ephesians 4:11-13, NIV. Emphasis mine.)

An equipping leader can recruit, train, and coach other leaders to do the ministry that builds up the church. This not only releases the church for exponential growth, but it also expands and matures the leadership base of the church.

Hiring a full-time youth pastor can bring a young and growing church to a screaming halt in other ways. Investing the limited resources of a new church into a full-time youth position can take away from the resources needed for outreach and evangelism. In a new church, teenagers will normally comprise about 5 to 10 percent of the population. But a new staff position can easily take up 20-25 percent of the annual budget. While we would expect a return on investment from any staff position, investing that much of your budget into an area with limited growth potential can be crippling to the overall mission of a church. Yes, the day will come when you should hire a youth pastor. But not quite yet.

We recommend that your first hire should be a part-time specialist focusing on the areas of worship, children's ministry, or administration. Why? There are three reasons (1) These ministries directly affect Sunday morning ministry, and as Sunday morning goes, so goes the rest of the week in a new church plant. (2) Most church planters are young and inexperienced in hiring and managing staff. It is a lot easier to start off with part-timers than full-timers. (3) It is simply more cost-effective when you are operating on limited resources. One of the best hires I ever made was a part-time worship leader who added twice the value at one-third the cost of a full-time employee.

If you are going to hire a full-time person, we recommend that you hire a generalist, a leader who can oversee and equip leaders in several areas of the ministry. Dave Gwartney of Christ Church of Wrigleyville in Chicago, Illinois brought on a great full-time staff person, Jon Klinepeter. Jon is an equipping leader. He has recruited leaders and built teams throughout this new church in the areas of worship, children's ministry, programming, communications, along with sharing the teaching load on Sunday morning. This is a key reason their new church has smashed the 200 barrier in attendance and is working towards breaking the 400 barrier.

Settling for What You Can Afford

There are no blue-light specials when it comes to finding exceptional people. Pat MacMillan, in his book *Hiring Excellence* (NavPress, © 1992), writes, "We are often too quick to settle for acceptable versus exceptional ones!" Too many churches and pastors simply settle for what they can afford

Churches look for:	Impact Players want:
• Stability	• Excitement
• Structure	• Flexibility
• Subordinates	• Partnerships
• Saving money	• Compensation
• Someone to shape	• To shape others

rather than waiting for or paying more for that impact player they need for reaching their ministry goals. We would rather see church planters hire a volunteer from the inside who is a known commodity than to try to cut a deal with an outsider whose impact is unknown. If that volunteer doesn't exist, and you are forced to go outside, here are a few things you should consider regarding those who can really make a difference.

Most churches don't attract exceptional leaders. Actually, they tend to chase them away for a number of reasons. Churches tend to want stability. They don't want people to change things or to shake things up too fast. Impact players want excitement. They want to be part of creating something new and fresh. They desire to take risks and learn from their failures. They like walking on the edge, but churches tend to put up barriers. Churches tend to desire structure, but impact players want flexibility. They want the ability to create, change, and build their ministry. Churches want subordinates, but impact players are looking for partnerships. They want to be respected for their past achievements and for the expertise they provide. They want to be brought into the inner circle and asked their opinion on critical issues facing the ministry. They are not just looking to be a hired hand brought on to accomplish a task.

Churches are always looking to save money, but impact players want compensation. Impact players are experienced enough to sniff out cheapness in any church. No one goes into the ministry for the financial perks, but impact players want to be recognized for their contributions and want to know that their family is going to be cared for by receiving quality benefits, such as retirement, health care, and adequate vacations. Churches desire to shape someone, while an impact player wants to shape others. Impact players want to hear about the opportunities to influence others and contribute to the overall vision of the ministry.

Developing a Process for Hiring

Many church planters are intuitive leaders. The ability to make decisions internally is great for getting things started from scratch, but it can be a detriment as the church grows. Having healthy systems with workable processes is critical to the organization. This is crucial when it comes to the area of hiring staff, because going on a hunch or a gut decision could set off a landmine that may needlessly wound the new church. I look at process as a way of confirming the hunches of intuitive leaders. Consequently, I've developed a 12-step process based on these four questions:

What do they look like?

Where do you find them?

What do you do when they are in front of you?

How do you make the decision?

The Work of Hiring

What do they look like?

1. Preparing
2. Planning
3. Profiling

Where do you find them?

10. Tracking
11. Evaluating
12. Calling

Impact Player

4. Gathering
5. Networking
6. Recruiting

How do you make the decision

7. Interviewing
8. Referencing
9. Assessing

What do you do when they are in front of you?

1. What Do They Look Like?

a. Preparing

Every church must go through a process of preparing themselves for a new staff person. They need to take a fresh look at aligning their resources in the right direction to accomplish their vision. They need to count the cost and make the commitment to pay the price to get there as an organization. My boss, Bernie Tanis, led the executive board that hired me to purposefully provide the revenue necessary to see the vision of planting churches become a reality. They had counted the cost and were willing to pay the price to see their vision fulfilled. Too many churches and organizations settle for second best. We like what Dwight Eisenhower once said: "There are no victories at bargain prices."

b. Planning

Not only do you have to do a gut check to prepare yourself as a church, but you also need a plan that involves a strategic team to work through all the steps of the hiring process. We encourage you to look for people with spiritual wisdom and discernment, people with a knack for details, people with human resource experience, and people who know you well enough to give you honest feedback. One of the greatest gifts ever given to me was a man who came to Christ in our church plant. He had over twenty years' experience in human resource work in a large corporation in our area. One day I took him out to breakfast and said that I would teach him everything I knew about the Bible if he would teach me what he knew about recruiting, screening, hiring, and managing staff. This gift is still paying off great dividends to this day. He was on my team for every hire I made while I was at that church and was on the search team that looked for my successor. Planning involves not only getting the right people around you but also preparing the team by showing them how this hire is consistent with the vision of the church and helping with understanding the complete hiring process.

c. Profiling

The next step is determining a profile of your potential staff. This involves describing the type of person you need along with an adequate job description. Be sure to focus on the character qualities of 1 Timothy 3:1-10 and Titus 1:5-16, and translate these into measurable values. It's very interesting that a lot of those biblical qualifications deal with emotional health and relational abilities. Too often we get caught up with a person's talent or technical skills and neglect taking a hard look at their attitudes, work habits, and relational skills. John Maxwell gave some great advice in one of his monthly tapes from the Injoy Life Club. Here are the basics of what he looks for in a new staff member:

Makes things happen

Sees and seizes opportunities

Has a positive influence on others

Adds value

Attracts good people

Equips leaders

Provides ideas

Has a great attitude

Finishes well

Understands loyalty
(John Maxwell, *Searching For Eagles*, Injoy Life Club Vol.10, No. 6)

Profiling also involves developing a good job description. Good job descriptions empower leaders to lead by delegating specific responsibilities to staff and not simply dumping duties on them. Having a job description that empowers is critical to finding, attracting, and keeping good candidates. In *Seven Habits of Highly Effective People*, (Free Press, © 1990), Steven Covey provides a description the five elements of good delegation:

Desired Result – States a clear picture and mutual understanding on what needs to be accomplished.

Guidelines — Identifies the parameters within which the individual should operate. What not to do. What to do.

Resources — Identifies all the resources the person can draw on to accomplish the desired results.

Accountability — Sets up standards of performance and specific times for reporting/evaluation.

Rewards/Consequences — Identifies what will specifically happen, good or bad, as a result of the evaluation.

When developing a job description, exercise caution so that it does not become too idealistic or unrealistic. It should be flexible and expandable as the candidate grows into the job and the position evolves. Periodic updates to the job description show value for the employee and will help clarify expectations as your work relationship grows. An empowering job description will also be used to evaluate the employee's performance. It becomes an objective standard that guides and protects your relationship into the future.

2. Where Do You Find Them?

a. Gathering

Gathering a good base of potential staff candidates is essential to the hiring process. Too many churches and organizations make a decision on a critical staff position after considering just one qualified candidate. Pat MacMillan calls this a "binary trap." He writes,

> In decision-making theory, a binary trap is a yes or no answer to a single alternative. And it is just that — a trap! The quality of your decision can be no better than the best alternative on your list. If you have only one candidate, you'd better pray that that person is the best candidate, and very often he or she is not. (*Hiring Excellence* [NavPress, © 1992], p. 227)

To save yourself from this binary trap, you need to embrace the three elements of gathering: spotting potential, remembering potential, and drawing out potential. Spotting potential staff members is always on the mind of good leaders. And good leaders never forget an impact player. They know how to collect information and keep track of their whereabouts. Many times finding the right staff person is simply a matter of timing.

Churches that make good hiring moves know how to create interest in the position they are looking to fill. Whether placing ads in periodicals, utilizing Internet sites, or visiting seminaries, they know who they are looking for and what can move that person to respond. In some cases this might take 200 to 300 inquiries before three quality candidates emerge. One hint: to write good ads that attract people, make the first sentence in the form of a question that resonates and sticks in the heart of the reader. "Feeling stifled in your creative expression?" is better than "Seeking experienced worship pastor."

b. Networking

Networking is all about initiating relationships and connecting with people who can assist you in finding the candidates you need. Begin by creating a list of people who know people. Think though all the pastors, leaders, professors, and lay leaders you know and send out an email with a profile and job description attached. Give them a clear picture of what you are looking for. Once you get a lead, act within 24 to 48 hours. Strike while the iron is hot. This not only helps you find the right candidate, it communicates value to your network. I have one warning: Do your homework! Not everyone in your network is a good judge of talent and character. Sometimes leads are casually given because the person is simply a friend who needs a job—or they're less than a friend and are looking for a way to move them out of their current situation.

c. Recruiting

Some of the best candidates already have work. They're not seeking you; you're seeking them. This requires the skill of recruiting, and here are a few insights:

(1) Recruit to a vision, not just to a job. You've maybe heard the story of how Steven Jobs recruited John Sculley to move from PepsiCo to Apple Computers. The clincher wasn't salary — it was vision. Jobs said, "Mr. Sculley, do you want to sell sugared water the rest of your life, or do you want to come and change the world?" The type of people you want to work for you are people who have a passion to change the world, not just people who are looking for employment. You will need to have a clear and compelling vision that strikes at the basic needs of every human being — the needs for significance, for community, and for adventure. All leaders want to be part of something bigger than themselves, something that is making a difference. Your ability to paint a picture of the future that moves leaders at the core of their being will make the difference between getting average and excellent candidates.

(2) Change your posture. Too many recruiters think it is their job to protect the organization, and they end up taking a defensive posture. After Bible school I was looking for an organization to plant a church with.

I had been part of two independent church starts and sensed the need to be part of something bigger. I called every national denomination office I could work with theologically. Most calls were discouraging because the people I talked with took defensive positions. But one man, Vic Winquist, took my call and asked me questions about my dreams and desires. After a pleasant lunch meeting, he referred me to Larry Sieffert, a regional leader, who took the same posture. Sixteen years later, I've been part of seeing 50 churches started and hundreds of church planters trained, in part because some "old-timers" listened to, cared for, and asked relational questions of a young man with big dreams and little experience.

(3) Don't oversell. Wise candidates are turned off when they sense the recruiter moving from vision casting to selling a pipe dream. Be careful not to promise anything that is not in your control to deliver.

(4) Remember: the more qualified the candidate is, the longer it is going to take for him or her to make a decision. Good candidates are going to kick the tires for a while. They are going to check out the organization. Such candidates will make a decision that will affect a lot of people, so it is important not to rush or pressure them.

3. What Do You Do When They Are in Front of You?

a. Interviewing

There are three types of interviews needed for hiring: general screening, attitudes and skill competency, and character discernment.

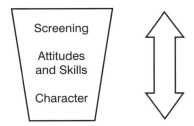

A screening interview typically happens on the phone, following a review of the candidate's resume or application. The interviewer is looking for first impressions and to see if the candidate truly meets the qualifications of the position. Questions are clarified and next steps are determined.

The second interview is a face-to-face meeting designed to determine competency, compatibility, and chemistry. Do they have the skills and attitudes to get the job done? Does their vision coincide with that of the church? Are they someone you would like to hang out with? Remember, questions from history reveal more than questions of preference.

Example of Face-to-face Interview Question

Criteria: Can the candidate make things happen?

Questions:

> Tell us about your proudest accomplishment in your current job.
>
> Describe a time where you were faced with limited resources and still got the job done.

The third interview is also a face-to-face interview, but this time it is essential that the spouse also attend. Again, open-ended questions are used, especially to reveal more about the candidate's character, Christian walk, and calling to vocational ministry. By this time your reference work, background checks, and diagnostic testing should have been completed. Any red flags can be addressed in this context.

Example of Candidate/Spouse Interview Question

Criteria: How vibrant is the candidate's spiritual life?

Questions:

> Describe to us how you stay fresh in your walk with Jesus.
>
> Tell about a time when you went through a spiritual drought and how you came out of it.
>
> Which part of Scripture are you focused on right now in your devotional life?

The number one interviewing mistake is failure to prepare. This is disrespectful; it breeds distrust in the minds of candidates and fosters a lack of confidence in the leader they are expected to follow. Data collecting is crucial to interviewing. If you are not a detail person, include detail people in the interview. Taking good notes reveals competence and seriousness. Don't talk too much, and don't be afraid of awkward moments of silence. Remember that the candidate is the featured speaker in the room and give him or her your undivided attention. Please turn off your cell phone, and make sure no phone calls get through. Setting the right tone and atmosphere is more important than some might think. Maintain the same positive, affirming posture that has been part of the recruitment process from the beginning.

b. Referencing

We check references because the best indicator of future behavior is past behavior. One referencing axiom is that the higher the position, more references are needed. There are three types of references that you can use to collect information: a standard form mailed back to you, a face-to-face interview, and a telephone interview. The best is the face-to-face interview, but the most practical is the phone interview.

Here are some ideas to help you get the most from reference calls: (1) Develop good questions based upon the profile you have developed. If one of the criteria is "makes things happen" then develop questions to address that issue: "How would you describe their energy level?" "What project would not have happened without them?" (2) Make sure the questions are open-ended, and cannot easily be answered with a yes or no. This will help the person feel at ease and speak freely about the candidate's qualifications. Many times people speak so freely that they give you information that you were not even probing for. (3) In some cases, practice the "two deep" rule: ask the references for others you may contact. "Could you recommend anyone else who would be able to give us further insight into the candidate's qualifications for this position?"

c. Assessing

Assessment refers to a combination of third-party sign-offs, background checks, and diagnostic testing. A third-party sign-off means that some form of objective input from others factors into the hire. This protects you from the "falling in love" syndrome of hiring, where you may have prematurely made a commitment in your mind to hire this person. Having people in your corner who have a good track record in hiring can save you from a lot of pain. Bring such people in on the last interview, or bring them in on an informal lunch interview. Don't become defensive when a candidate's shortcomings are exposed.

Background checks include criminal, financial, and education verification. For less than $50.00 you can get clear objective information from a number of sources. By getting a candidate's permission, you get an invaluable window into their lives. It seems outlandish, but many churches have been burned by pastors who have claimed to have degrees from institutions they have never attended! A look at one's financial dealings uncovers personal discipline and strong fiscal responsibility—or possibly lapses of integrity. There is a strong correlation between poor hires and poor fiscal responsibility.

Diagnostic testing involves job compatibility profiles, work style assessments, and personality profiles. Here are two helpful tools:

    Job Perceptions Inventory: Developed by Dr. John G. Geier and Dorothy E. Downey, this inventory provides a profile of what the candidate perceives the job to be as well as what is required to perform well in the position. The person hiring the individual also takes the inventory to provide a benchmark. If there are extreme differences in the perceptions of what the job is and what it takes to succeed in it, further discussion may be necessary.

Portrait Predictor: The Portrait Predictor is a personality instrument to identify one's preferred operational style using the DISC format (Direct, Inspire, Support and Correct). An easy-to-understand, concise report that summarizes a person's observable behavior is provided. It shows:

Portrait Theme (the most prominent D-I-S-C characteristic) and Descriptor (representing the particular mix of D-I-S-C)

D-I-S-C basic characteristics

Description: a paragraph highlighting the behavioral tendencies

Strengths: the strongest characteristics

Growth Areas: what needs to be addressed, especially when working with people with other DISC patterns

Style Overview: one sentence on each of these areas: teaming, focus, frustrations, motivated by, threatened by

Additional comments, aimed at enhancing relations with others: Comfort Zone, Challenge Zone, Coaching Cue, and Key Questions to Ask

4. How Do You Make the Decision?

a. Tracking

Tracking is simply keeping a running scorecard of each candidate. This scorecard is built around the profile and job description that you and your team have developed. If you don't know what you are aiming at, you will never hit it. One suggestion is to integrate a rating system of 1 to 5 into the profile. Take clear, understandable, objective notes. Church planters are notorious for overlooking objectivity, and they often get wounded when they do! Have all the data in one place: resume, references, background checks, diagnostic tools, and interview notes.

b. Evaluating

During the evaluation phase, all data on the top three candidates are collected and collated on the running scorecards. Those responsible for the final hiring decision should then consider "the seven C's":

Does the job fit them? (Competency)

Do they fit the job? (Compatibility)

Do they fit the organization? (Chemistry)

Can we afford them? (Compensation)

Can we trust them? (Character)

Do we see Jesus in them? (Christian Walk)

Why do they want to work here? (Call)
(Based on Pat MacMillan, *Hiring Excellence*, pp. 81-101)

If you cannot answer these questions positively about any given candidate, don't hire that person!

c. Deciding

Finally the decision is made. You have bathed this process in prayer and have had many others praying, too. You have, to the best of your ability, worked the process and have made your choice. And yet your job is not finished. This is where you need to keep your head in the game and do a good job of calling this individual to be a part of your team. Here are some suggestions to guide you in effectively calling this person:

Notify the candidate of your decision in person, if at all possible. Otherwise call him or her on the phone.

Follow this conversation by writing a personal letter extending the invitation to them and celebrating this milestone in their lives.

Provide an updated job description, clearly outlining your expectations and reporting systems. Also include a clear outline of the salary, benefits, and moving expenses.

Provide your employee policy manual if you have one.

Send out special announcements to the right people, especially those who will be directly working with or reporting to the new hire.

Hold an installation service. Celebrate this moment in their lives and in the life of the church. The rule here is: If you can't celebrate their hiring, then don't hire them!

Prepare current staff and volunteers for the new hire. There might be people under his or her leadership who need some tender-loving care as they come to grips with the decision. Be there for them until the staff person wins them over.

Let them go and stay out of the way. If you don't trust them to do the job, don't hire them. Give them space and freedom to do their job within the appropriate reporting systems.

There is an old saying: "Hire hard. Manage Easy." The work of hiring is painfully slow for church planters who are used to making decisions on the fly and trusting their intuition. Hiring your first staff person from the outside is like entering a dangerous minefield. Caution and care are needed to navigate it. Peter Drucker observes

> Fast personnel decisions are likely to be wrong decisions. Among the effective executives I have had the occasion to observe, there have been people who make decisions fast, and people who make them slowly. But without exception, they make personnel decisions slowly, and they make them several times before they really commit themselves. (*The Effective Executive*, [MacMillan, © 2002], pp. 32)

If you hire easy, chances are that you are going to end up managing hard. This is grief that you don't need. Col. Earl "Red" Blaik, the legendary Army football coach, describes what happens when we get it right. "Once in a while you are lucky enough to have the thrill and satisfaction of working with a group of men who are willing to make every sacrifice to achieve a goal, and then experience the achievement of it with them. In this, believe me, there is a payment that cannot be matched in any other pursuit."

Other Resources: *Pat MacMillan, Hiring Excellence: Six Steps to Making Good People Decisions*, NavPress, 1992

Robert W. Wendover, *Smart Hiring: The Complete Guide to Finding and Hiring the Best Employees*, Sourcebooks, Inc., 2002

John Maxwell, *Staffing Excellence, 10 Audio Lessons on Hiring, Motivating, Evaluating your Team, www.Injoy.com*

Questions to Ponder (While Standing in This Minefield)

Where have I seen owner/employee tension?

Are there people from within who are worthy of consideration?

Who can help me make objective hiring decisions?

What issues might I naturally overlook?

How will we pray about our hiring process?

LANDMINE 10:

DELAYING MISSION ENGAGEMENT

Glory built on selfish principles is shame and guilt.
William Cowper

I have yet to meet a church planter who admits, "I really have a dream of just sort of starting my church and kind of just growing it and leaving it at that. I don't really have an interest in seeing that church participate in the broader mission opportunities of the Kingdom of God". Church planters who do have that mindset should admit it; they'd save their superiors the agony of asking them when they intend to get around to participating in the broader mission of building God's Kingdom.

That may sound cynical. Most church planters do feel and say the right things at the front end of their church planting pilgrimage. Some are grandiose: "I intend to start a church that reproduces itself. ... I want to have a church planting church. ... I want to see our church play a role in the broader movement of our denomination." Some are less grandiose, but at least they agree to be part of the movement. None are ever opposed to a reproducing movement; that would be like being opposed to prayer! They even put it into their vision and value statements. They teach their launch team members and early leaders that this is why the new church exists. And all nod their heads. But somewhere along the way diversions occur or a shift of the heart takes place. This metamorphosis can take many forms:

Losing the vision to parent a new church

Failing to become a financially generous church

Being unwilling to participate in the broader mission of the denomination or sending agency

Ignoring cross-cultural or international missions

We'll do well to understand the roots—and then steer clear — of this landmine. It will be to your advantage to do so.

Too Weak, Too Strong, and the Curse of the "Y" Word

Diverging from an initial resolve to be a reproducing, Kingdom-oriented church can happen no matter how weak or strong the church may be. When a new church isn't as strong as quickly as the visionary leaders had envisioned, factual realities cloud their perspective. Finances are tighter than imagined and the workload is heavy. It's hard to think about being a generous church, giving away people and money and prayer for causes beyond their immediate concern. These churches perceive themselves to be too weak to get into the game.

But in other cases, just the opposite has happened. The church has grown strong enough—sometimes rapidly—to achieve a measure of health. Although the workload is substantial, finances are doing well, and the church has an upbeat attitude. Logically speaking, there's no reason for this church to ignore mission beyond its target area, but for some mysterious reason the "Y" word"—yet – appears: "We're not ready quite yet to give...sacrifice...take risks." The church wants to add a staff member or purchase land or some other noble cause. And they are good causes. It's just that sometimes the good is the enemy of the best. The trouble is that the "Y" word eventually becomes the "WHY?" word. People forget their vision and present realities suffocate the dream.

We have seen it time and time again. It reminds me of the farmer who is asked by a neighbor to lend him some rope. "Sorry," he says, "I'm using my rope to tie up my milk." The neighbor protests, "Hey, you don't need rope to tie up milk!" The farmer says, "Well, any excuse is a good one when you don't want to do something."

The challenge here is to not submit to fear or drift from the parameters of the Great Commission: "Then Jesus came to them again and said, 'All authority in heaven and on earth has been given to me. Therefore go and make disciples of all nations, baptizing them in the name of the Father and of the Son and of the Holy Spirit, and teaching them to obey everything I have commanded you. And surely I am with you always to the very end of the age' " (Matthew 28:18-20). This charge carries with it the command to do the work of mission as well as the promise of authority and the presence of Christ.

Then, before the ascension, Jesus said this: "But you will receive power when the Holy Spirit comes on you; and you will be my witnesses in Jerusalem, and in all Judea and Samaria, and to the ends of the earth" (Acts 1:8). That text is an outline verse for the Book of Acts. It describes the natural progression of the church in Jerusalem (chapters 1-7), moving through Judea and Samaria (chapters 8-12), and then to the ends of the earth (chapters 13-28). It is both descriptive and prescriptive in nature. Paul's epistles consistently call the churches that already exist to play a role in the broadening expansion of God's Kingdom.

Thus, we can define a missional church as one that joyfully plays a sacrificial role in the growth of God's work at home, cross-culturally, and abroad.

Reasons to Be a Missional Church

For leaders of young churches who need reminding, I offer the following two compelling reasons to fight hard to fashion your church into a missional church.

1. Our theology requires it.

Read what I just wrote about the Great Commission. And who can argue with Paul, when writing to the church at Corinth, who held up the churches in northern Greece (Macedonia) as examples of missional participation? "And now, brothers, we want you to know about the grace that God has given the Macedonian churches. Out of the most severe trial, their overflowing joy and extreme poverty welled up in rich generosity. For I testify that they gave as much as they were able, and even beyond their ability. Entirely on their own they urgently pleaded with us for the privilege of sharing in this service to the saints" (2 Corinthians 8:1-4). That obliterates the "too weak" argument, doesn't it?

2. God blesses generosity.

That sounds familiar. I worked this theme quite a bit in the chapter on fear of money issues, and here I go again. One thing that really gets me steamed is when leaders of new churches encourage their members to be generous ("because God blesses generosity"), but then they hold their fists tightly when it comes to creating a church budget that is generous toward mission.

The same principle of generosity being blessed applies to both individuals and institutions, such as churches. Churches that give are churches that are blessed. That blessing can be manifested in many ways: corporate enthusiasm, financial needs being met, numerical growth, and relational wholeness.

I recently asked Steve Scheller, a missionary recruiter with Mission: Moving Mountains (Minneapolis) for his perspective on this issue. He routinely interacts with hundreds of churches, both new and established, regarding their participation in global missions. His perspective is consistent with what I've seen.

> One example of a young but missional church is Hope Community Church in Minneapolis, pastored by Steve Treichler. It's a church of about 300-400. They started supporting us financially in 2002 or 2003, and have also sent people to join our mentoring team in Nigeria. In the last year or so, this fairly new church that had been

renting a facility from an older church, was given a building, equipment, parking lot, and fleet of vehicles for FREE. It's prime downtown real estate worth many millions, exponentially beyond what they first laid out in faith to missions.

I have a database of approximately 1,600-,2000 contacts at any given time. Over the years I have heard pastors share two perspectives. One is "We love your cause, but we have too many needs in our own community to recruit people or give to missions right now," or "Our own community is our mission." The second perspective which seems more rare, is "Wow, you have a great mission. Because we have so many needs in our own community and we are called to be world Christians, we want to give to worldwide missions." And these congregations, perhaps not all to the degree of Hope Community Church, seem to be blessed! We have a missionary God who is moving His Spirit among the nations, and it seems that when we get in touch with what His Spirit is doing in the world, we tend to catch the wind also for what he is doing locally and are blessed beyond our wildest imaginations.

3. Obligation and Integrity

Here's a word we don't run into too often in our Christian subculture: obligation. I'm speaking of obligation to the ones who made your journey possible: a parent church, your denomination, your sending agency. In all likelihood you joined with a family that had a dream for you. The dream was to be a reproducing church that contributed to the broader efforts of the organization. Many prayed, many gave, to see your dream fulfilled.

I'm not here to promote a dysfunctional family system that is characterized by guilt and codependence. We know that we can't please everyone. But there's a positive side to obligation, too. Paul wrote, "I am obligated both to Greeks and non-Greeks, both to the wise and the foolish. That is why I am so eager to preach the gospel also to you who are in Rome" (Romans 1:14-15). Or, "If anyone does not provide for his relatives, and especially for his immediate family, he has denied the faith and is worse than an unbeliever" (1 Timothy 5:8). There are certain responsibilities that come with the territory of being an apostle. There are certain responsibilities with being a parent or a wage-earner. And there are certain responsibilities that new churches bear to participate in mission.

I was at a denominational celebration banquet once where the speaker, Pastor John Jenkins of First Baptist Church of Glenarden, Maryland, was chiding new churches for their lack of participation in mission. Pastor Jenkins is a church planting leader among the African-American community in the

Washington, D.C. area (see chapter 5). He pastors the largest church in our denomination. He understands both obligation and opportunity. He said,

> Paul wrote in Philippians 4:15, "In the early days of your acquaintance with the gospel...not one church shared with me in the matter of giving and receiving, except you only" What a tragedy that there are churches who will receive the support from churches or a denomination and then refuse to give support back to the very hand that fed them! To receive from someone and then not give back is a shame and disgrace to the Kingdom. Paul applauds the Philippians that they gave to and supported his ministry, and he was disappointed with those whom he had served who chose not to send him support!

Further you have an obligation to follow your original mission statement as best you can. Remember your original intent? You were among those who were trusting God to make your church into a Kingdom force. Maybe the going started to get tough, but that doesn't mean that you can diverge from your course too quickly. In fact, some churches find that it is at the moment that they put a foot in the water that the Red Sea is held back.

Pastor Chad Huff, of Rivercity Community Church in Kansas City, Missouri, learned how difficult planting a church can be. He originally targeted the up-and-coming, upwardly mobile young executives that a resurgent downtown was attracting. But God was bringing a much broader spectrum of people than that. Sure, there were the young executives, but there were the homeless and everything in between. While the methodology of Rivercity necessarily changed, its vision of being a positive influence in its community and beyond never wavered. It remained generous toward the needy and generous toward planting new churches. It stayed the course and supported denominational endeavors. And then—out of the blue—a church that was closing its doors after nearly 100 years of ministry gave Rivercity their building, valued at $1.4 million. Says Chad, "I wonder if God would have blessed us if we would have given up on our core values too soon."

4. The Need

The final reason I submit for keeping your young church on track as a missional church is the undeniable need all over the world. Yes, the need in your specific target community or group is huge, too, but the broader call still beckons. "During the night Paul had a vision of a man of Macedonia standing and begging him, 'Come over to Macedonia and help us' "(Acts 16:10). Simply speaking, we need every church to participate in the broader mission. Some estimates say that in the United States we close between 3,000 and 4,000 churches each year while planting less than 2,000.

Ways to Maintain Your Missional Commitment

Some people compare being a missional church to raising a family: (1) There's never an ideal time to start doing so. (2) There are always sufficient reasons to delay the action: not enough money, not enough time, not enough whatever. Although we count the cost and determine when to start raising a family, we don't have the privilege of counting the cost when we start to obediently do what God calls us to do. As leaders, we lead our churches to do what is right… at the moment. The good news is that, as in raising a family, pushing our churches toward mission usually has a way of working out in the long run. What are some specific applications to lead in this direction?

1. Plant a Daughter Church

As I stated earlier, nearly every church planter that we meet speaks sincerely and intentionally of planting a church that will, in turn, plant other churches. It's an irony of church planting that after the new church launches to public services, it begins a long season of being inwardly focused. Strange, isn't it? The church piles its resources into "getting healthy enough," but like the elusive Holy Grail, "healthy" is always just out of reach. That's particularly true of churches that are knocking at the door of the "200 barrier"—churches that have about 200 people in attendance. C. Peter Wagner used to call that size church "the awkward church," because vision is always outstripped by available resources.

Missional churches count the cost of truly fulfilling their mission, but they are not intimidated by that cost. One church planter put a "birth before we build" statement right into the new church's vision and value documentation. It became a teaching point at every membership class. In the church I planted, we continuously announced our goal of having our church become a parent church by our third birthday.

And it happened! We were so oblivious to the challenge that God blessed us by sending us an equally oblivious church planter who took the challenge of our under-resourced, under-informed toddler church. He and his wife went on to plant an incredible church in a nearby community. Their names? Gary and Mary Rohrmayer.

If you said you were going to be a reproducing church, put a plan in motion right away to get there. From day one, set aside a portion of your church's income toward church planting. Keep speaking the language. I used to say to people who were moving away, "We're not going to pray that you find a good church; we're going to pray that you help start a good church!" (As a matter of fact, that's how our first daughter church, planted by the Rohmayers, was initiated. We had a young family move to Oconomowoc, Wisconsin, and they called me saying, "O.K., find a church planting couple and we'll help them start a church!)In another instance a church mobilized its high school ministry to do the groundwork of starting a new church. They did the demographic work, took surveys, visited established churches, and performed prayer walks in anticipation of a new church starting. After a year of persistent work a church planting couple was recruited to start the new work.

Another way to get the ball rolling is to attract church planting interns. I recently received a letter from Mike and Janet Holba, church planters at Ripon Community Church in Ripon, Wisconsin. They were requesting all of their financial supporters phase out their financial support—but would they please reallocate their support toward their new church planting interns. We had done the same thing when we planted, and that gave us our second church planting couple to deploy. Internships are a workable strategy to get potential church planters into the game while keeping the vision of being a reproducing church always in front of the church you're planting.

You can do it! Set faith goals. Believe God for the extraordinary. Don't succumb to fear, and be careful of using the "yet" word. Keep telling your new church, "We're all just one generation away from the extinction of the church, unless we continue to plant new ones. We can't become the last link in the chain of Christianity!"

2. Be Generous

At least be a church that tithes. Allocate at least 10 percent of your offerings and budget to missional causes outside of your direct concern. And don't wait! That's like waiting to be obedient until a more appropriate time.

This past summer my sixteen-year-old son got his first job, working at a fast-food restaurant. Like many young men, he had his sights set on getting his first automobile. So I made him a deal. I would match his savings, up to a certain point, as long as he was tithing. He thought it was a pretty good deal— a 100 percent return on investment after an initial 10 percent sacrifice.

I think I made a good decision when I made him the offer, and he thinks so, too. For one, he has been spiritually blessed by supporting an underprivileged child in a third-world nation through his tithing. He has been thrilled to be a primary source of supply for this boy in another land. But there's more. A few days ago he purchased his car—with the unexpected help of his grandfather. The result is that he has a very nice car, far beyond what he imagined, because God blessed him spiritually and financially.

My point is this: don't delay being a generous church. Be that way from the beginning, and demonstrate to your people that there are certain things that we don't compromise on. One church that we helped plant is notoriously strapped for money. So they don't give. So…they're strapped for money. This often becomes a vicious cycle.

I like the attitude of Dr. Stu Dix, who pastors First Baptist Church in Darlington, Wisconsin. His church is in farming country, and it has a reputation for being generous, starting many new churches and helping whomever they can. A couple of years ago his treasurer approached him with some alarming news: the checkbook balance had fallen below $50,000. Stu's response was classic. "Good!" he told the treasurer. "Let me know when we're below $5,000. I'll be glad to see our church be as generous as we can until we have to depend on God again!"

3. Participate in the Life of the Denomination or Sending Agency

You can choose your friends, but you can't choose your family." I suppose that's true for people, but it's not precisely true for new churches that have been birthed through a denominational family. In most cases church planters are part of the denomination or organization because they wanted to be; there was theological consistency and mutually perceived value in forging the alliance. So church planters choose both their friends and their family. In the long run, this can be a tremendously rewarding and effective relationship. The corporate strength of the denomination works to start new churches; the new churches participate to strengthen the denomination. And, as a seminary professor used to remind me, "Sooner or later your church will get into trouble. That's why you need to be affiliated with someone who can help you when the going gets tough."

The challenge for leaders of a new church is to walk the tightrope between loyalty to the denomination and understanding that there is a long courtship process to bring unchurched people into a positive relationship with the denomination. The process of assimilation can look like this:

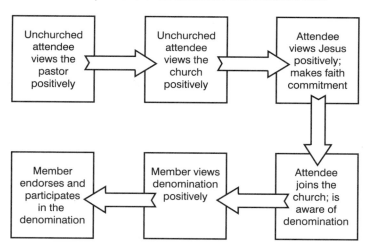

What I'm illustrating is that I fully realize that it takes a while for new attendees to embrace their new denomination. It's a progression, and it would be wrong to push loyalty to the denomination too soon. I've heard of denominational executives who show up at the grand opening of a new church to publicly welcome the new attendees to their new affiliation. Perhaps that's going overboard. But the opposite extreme is to bury an affiliation so far down in the paperwork that people have no clue that this church has a broader family. In our movement we do not require the use of a denominational name in advertising, but we do require that the name show up in literature (such as the bulletin) so that newcomers are aware of our affiliation. And we don't allow new churches to use the term "nondenominational" or to advertise under that banner in the yellow pages of the telephone directory.

I am disturbed at how quickly some new churches disassociate themselves from their sponsoring denomination or agency. I guess it's like the teenager who doesn't want to admit that she has parents. She knows she needs her parents, but she doesn't want to incur a public relations dilemma by actually acknowledging them. However, the whole issue of denominationalism is much less of an issue today than it was even fifteen or twenty years ago. Missiologists are right when they say we're in a postmodern and postdenominational world. At one time we advertised, "This is not the church of your childhood!" But more and more people have no recollection of a childhood church. Denominational names are much less polarizing than they were a few years ago.

What are some ways to participate in the denomination? Raise up some of your people to serve on boards and committees. Send people to sponsored training events. Bring people to the annual meeting. Cooperate with leadership and honor them publicly and privately. Pray for them. Participate in special appeals and campaigns. Distribute literature and, where appropriate, allow the denomination access to your membership mailing lists. Live up to your commitments. Your denomination is a missions agency, so take advantage of the resource. You'll need them sooner or later. Trust me.

4. International Missions Involvement

My last suggestion for becoming a missional church is to expose your new church to international missions causes. The payoff for the world—and for your new church—can be incredible.

Getting involved in international mission is a lot easier than it might seem. This is one area where I failed as a church planter. Perhaps I was intimidated by the international scene, and my true focus was on church planting in the United States. But it was a mistake to shield my people from international missions. Thankfully, subsequent pastors at that church have brought the congregation into the blessing of international work. As the Bible says, "…to the ends of the earth."

Your denomination probably has opportunities that go beyond simple financial support of missionaries. There are short-term missions, special projects, and sponsorship opportunities. And there is a plethora of parachurch agencies that have legitimate and pressing needs. You hardly need to go looking for them, because they'll find you!

Short-term mission projects of a week or two can go a long way toward developing a missional mindset in your church. Participants come away with renewed vigor for missions both home and abroad. They also come away more supportive of the new church because of the depth of camaraderie that's been forged while enduring the rigors of the trip. And often these projects touch an emotional or sentimental chord that make fundraising relatively easy. Such projects end up giving the church a "larger than life" cause without affecting the budget.

My recommendation is to not delay. Leaders of new churches need to do whatever they can to imprint their church with a missional mindset. The DNA is formed in the earliest days, and the opportunity to design your church into a Kingdom-impact force will never be greater.

Questions to Ponder (While Standing in This Minefield)

What might cause our church to lose its missional dream?

Are we willing to trust God by becoming a generous church?

What communities or people groups will we target for a daughter church? When?

How can we get involved in international missions right now?

How can we honor our denominational leaders?

What am I afraid of?